THE SECRETS TO HOW NOT
TO THROW MAMA FROM THE TRAIN

BY JANICE HOOKER FORTMAN, Ed.D.

Thank You!

2019

The Secrets To How Not To Throw Mama From The Train
Copyright © 2016, Janice Fortman, Chicago, IL

ISBN-13: 978-0-9969396-1-4

Printed in the United States of America

To Place Orders Through JHFortman & Associates:
Website: www.speakersforalloccasions.com
Email: JHFortmanassociates@comcast.net
Telephone: 1-877-66-SPEAK (1-877-667-7325)

Acknowledgements

I would like to take this time to acknowledge all of the women who talked with me candidly about their relationships with their mothers. At times we laughed and at times we cried together. I would also like to thank my mother, whom I love dearly, for inspiring me to write this book.

I decided to write this book because I am an adult daughter with an aging mother. This relationship is one of the strongest bonds that exists between two people, is often very complicated and very few women openly discuss it. Often women feel if they complain about the relationship with their mothers, they are communicating disrespect, ungratefulness, etc. I am hoping this book can shed some light and offer some assistance, or even solutions, to having more pleasant and loving relationships between adult daughters and their aging mothers.

"The relationship between parents and children, but especially between mothers and daughters, is tremendously powerful, scarcely to be comprehended in any rational way." -- Joyce Carol Oates.

Table of Contents

Can I Get A Witness?

A Confession & Guide

Survey

From A Little Girl To A Woman

Hurts So Bad

It Wasn't About The Biscuits

Something Has To Change

Perceptions: What's Right?

A Little More Research

Can You Relate?

What's Wrong With The Way I Dress???!!!

Yo' Mama

The Letter

So What About Her Feelings?

How Your Behavior Affects Her Behavior

From Negative To Positive

Meetings Can Lead To Resolutions

I Can See Clearly

Save Yourself

The Little Bell

Reflections

Responses To Online Survey

Understanding Your Mother's Fear of Being Cast Aside

Who Is Yo' Mama?

Communication Commandments

Lordy, Lordy, I Have Become My Mother

Working Things Out

The Hand That Rocks The Cradle

Contradictions

Support Systems

Sisters & Mothers

Recognition

Is It Me or Is It Her?

Awareness

Caregiving

Bottom Line

Resources

Can I Get A Witness?

She's very independent, says anything without thinking of how what she says affects people. She's stubborn, insulting, controlling, spiteful, cantankerous, stressful and wants to be independent but is totally dependent on me. She loves her sons unconditionally, but barely tolerates her adult daughter. She tells her daughter how to dress, how to wear her hair, how to drive, how to raise her child, how she should spend her money, etc., etc., and so forth, and complains that her daughter never listens to her. She is 90 years old and I love her with all of my heart. She is my mama. I hate to admit it, and some people might be shocked, but wow, sometimes I feel like throwing mama from the train. Can I get a witness??!!

After I started relating my difficulties to some of my friends, to my surprise I discovered that there are many adult daughters who feel the same way. Often, the lists of concerns or problems were identical to mine – or eerily similar. I then started watching communication patterns of adult daughters and their mothers in various places, e.g., the grocery store, church, practically anywhere that I would see such interactions. Some of the situations I observed mirrored mine; most all I could relate to. So I decided that maybe I could write a book about my situation and other situations I saw or was told about. I began to wonder why this relationship is so difficult. Why is it so common? More importantly, why haven't I read about it? I decided to do some research, and found that although this relationship was identified as very complicated, there were not many articles, books or even research about it. When I spoke to a group of friends and women I didn't even know and told them that I had been thinking about writing a book about the relationship between adult daughters and their aging mothers, often I would hear "Wow! Please let me know when it comes out." "We need a book like this." "I will definitely read it"!

"Can I be in your book? But I want to be anonymous! "When I told one woman what I was writing about, she cornered me, invited me for a cup of coffee and said, "I have to get this off of my mind and you are a godsend." "You are a godsend!" Then she launched into her story.

"My mother and I have had a difficult relationship since the day I was born. Her friends (and mine) say the problem is that we're too much alike. It took a long time for me to understand this. I found out that mom was ignored by her mother and she was deeply affected by this. I was her first born. She had no mothering skills and knew only what her mother taught her - which was nothing - about raising a daughter. I guess my mom compensated by being overly controlling. She has said the most hurtful things to me and to be honest I can't pinpoint where it started or why she was always so upset with me."

As we were having coffee, another woman said that she didn't mean to, but had overheard our conversation and wanted to join in. She started telling her story. "I can relate to this situation but mine is totally different. I have tried over & over again to please my mother, which never works out because if it's not my mother's way then it's the highway. I don't understand why parents figure they can run your life forever or are never satisfied about anything. What's up with that?

For the past 4 weeks my mother and I have not spoken to each other. It started out with me being angry with her about her behavior towards me in front of some of my friends because I chose to go to a play that was not her choice."

"My mother gets on my nerves!"

"My mother is driving me crazy!"

I have discovered that this is an issue that is rarely discussed openly in mainstream culture, which makes those affected feel even more abnormal and isolated. I have also discovered that this issue of poor mother-daughter relationships is more common than uncommon.

A Confession & Guide

I must admit I am writing this self-help book as much for myself as for you. Since I have embarked on this journey, I have been noticing the dynamics between adult daughters and mothers in various places - grocery stores, department stores, movies, restaurants, church and other places. It's amazing to me that I had never paid any attention to this before I found myself in this situation. Why are some mothers and daughters enjoying each other while others are arguing, frowning, and just looking like if they could be anywhere else or with anybody else they would?

My goal for this book is to explore and offer some advice and techniques that have been shared with me from various women on how to have balance in this extremely complex relationship - and definitely "how not to throw mama from the train"! Remember, we can't change our mamas. The secret to a successful relationship is all in how we act in response to them.

Let's get started. I would like you to fill out the following questionnaire. It will help guide you through this book. I have distributed this survey/questionnaire to many women either by giving it to them personally or by publishing it online. Some scenarios and responses are my own, some were given by women I know and others were given anonymously via the survey. I used some of the suggestions and techniques that were related to my personal situation and found many to be successful. You may see your relationship in some of these scenarios. Hopefully, the suggestions, comments and techniques that are offered may help you strengthen your relationships. At the end of this book I will give you some results of the online survey.

Survey

1. How old are you? _____

2. How old is your mother (if living)? _____

3. How old was your mother if she has passed? _____

4. Are/were you a care giver? If so:

   a. Living in the same household _____

   b. Living in a different household _____

5. How long are/were you a caregiver? _____

6. What responsibilities do/did you have for your mother whether or not you are/were her caregiver?

   _____

   _____

   _____

   _____

   _____

7. How do you rate your relationship with your mother?

   a. Superior _____

   b. Excellent _____

   c. Satisfactory _____

   d. Unsatisfactory _____

8. If you rate your relationship as either (a) or (b) please briefly explain below.

   _____

   _____

   _____

_____

_____

9. If you rate your relationship as either (c) or (d) please briefly explain below.

_____

_____

_____

_____

_____

10. What one thing does your mother do/say that triggers strong negative feelings in you?

_____

_____

_____

_____

_____

11. What one thing does your mother do/say that triggers strong positive feelings in you?

_____

_____

_____

_____

_____

12. Do you feel that there are more positive feelings or negative feelings? _____

13. If you feel that there are more negative feelings, how do you cope?

_____

_____

_____

_____

_____

14. If you feel that there are more positive feelings, to what do you attribute this?   .

_____

_____

_____

_____

_____

15. Are there any comments/scenarios/funnies you would like to add?

_____

_____

_____

_____

_____

_____

_____

_____

_____

From A Little Girl To A Woman

The developmental issues an individual faces change over the course of the lifespan, from a young child's increasing need for autonomy to an older adult's possible increasing needs for care.

Let's examine the transition from a young female child to an adult woman. As a young child, daughters perceive their mothers as the safety net that provides their everyday basic physical needs such as nourishment, a feeling of safety and security and affection. As their daughters grow older, mothers become the person to help encourage self-esteem and self-identification. She becomes the role model for being female. What little girl hasn't tried on her mother's high heel shoes and jewelry, dressed in her clothing and put on her makeup?

My friend Loretta told me that one day, when her mother was at work, she decided to go into her mother's closet and try on her mother's favorite dress. She had to use a chair to stand on to get the dress off of the hanger. The dress was a bright red with long fitted sleeves and a white lace collar. She found safety pins to pin the dress on herself. Then she saw some pretty red shoes and, of course, she tried them on with the dress. Then she went to her mother's dressing table and put on makeup and red lipstick. As she said to me, "I looked like a Halloween mess. When my mother came home and saw me, I thought she was going to faint. Her eyes got big and she said, "Oh Lord, what have you done?" Then she said, "You are beautiful." I did not know until later that after she washed the makeup off of me, and unpinned the dress, she went into the room and cried. I had ruined her favorite dress!

As girls become teenagers, they need unconditional love, respect, support and validation from their mothers. A teenage girl usually wants her mother to be her best friend and still be unquestionably her mother above all else. As a girl grows into young adulthood, though, she begins to seek autonomy. She becomes less dependent on her mother and wants to make her own way. She still desires this connection with her mother but doesn't necessarily want to be like her. This is usually the period when the daughter sometimes sees her mother as old fashioned, and as less than understanding. How many times (when you were a teenager) did you say to your mother, "You just don't understand? That was way back then when you were young"?

As the daughter gets older and the mother ages, the mother daughter relationship and roles often reverse. The daughter becomes the mother and the mother is treated as a daughter. This is often when that already complicated relationship becomes even more complicated. The daughter begins to feel that she has to "take care" of her mother. She often feels that she has to give her mother advice, and has become her mother's safety net.

Case in point – when I take my mother grocery shopping, if she puts something in her cart that I don't think she should eat, I start lecturing her on why her choice is not healthy. One day, she wanted to cook some greens and wanted to season them with salt pork. Now for some who don't know what that is, it is a big chunk of pork that looks like bacon, and is saturated in salt. Salt crystals are all over the surface. She put it in the shopping cart, I took it out. She put another piece in when my back was turned, and when we got to the checkout counter, I took it out, with a lecture. The checkout lady stood with an amused look on her face at our exchange. "I am *your* mother. You are not *my* mother. Remember that! Now put it back in my cart!!!! You eat what you want and I will eat what I want." So like a dutiful daughter, I put it back in her cart with a huge exasperated sigh.

Now let's go through this same transition from the mother's perspective. From birth, she is responsible for her daughter's very existence. She provides all of the everyday basic physical needs including love and nurturing. She loves, nurtures, advises, guides, encourages and supports her daughter. As the daughter becomes a teenager, mom begins to see that her daughter is being more independent and sometimes struggles to give that independence to the daughter. She wants to be her daughter's best friend, but still wants her daughter to realize that she is going to preserve her motherly role.

Holly related this scenario to me about her teenage daughter. "My daughter was very shy when she was a 16-year-old. I would encourage her to make friends, go bowling with her classmates (always with chaperones), and after her social outings, we would discuss what happened, just like two best friends. I saw her getting more independent and was happy about it. Or so I thought. Until she decided that she no longer wanted me to go shopping with her and help her pick out her clothes. I found myself saying, 'I am your mother, this is my money, and I am going to choose the clothes that I think are appropriate'. During an argument one day, she said something to me that stopped me in my tracks. She said 'Mom, you will always be my mother, but sometimes I want you to be my friend and let me find my own independence. You've already taught me how to dress appropriately. Please let me try on my own.'"

As the daughter gets older, the mother's need to become the adviser and guide often gets stronger because the daughter is growing more independent. When the daughter becomes an adult, mothers sometimes feel abandoned, especially when the daughter begins to pull away, does not feel the need to follow mother's advice anymore, overtly asserts her self-determination, and even purposely ignores or goes against her mother's advice and opinions.

Although the daughter wants her independence, she still wishes to keep her connection with her mother However, often the mother does not easily give up that role and unfortunately, this is where the relationship gets antagonistic and confrontational. The daughter may feel that mom is controlling and maybe still treating her like a child, while mother may still feel the need to guide the daughter's path.

When the daughter gets married, has children, prefers to socialize with her peers and mother is no longer the center of the daughters life, often, as a result, some mothers feel they are being rejected and excluded from their daughter's lives. They feel they have been replaced! You will find such examples in many of the pages to follow.

Hurts So Bad

I want to be specific on why I felt that this book would be important to lots of adult daughters. I can do this by revealing what happened in my relationship with my mother and by sharing a few specific occurrences. I cannot say that I have all of the answers, but here are some scenarios from my relationship with my mom.

My mother felt that I was not raising my only son correctly. "You are too lenient. You should not allow him to wear his hair like that. I would not help him buy a car. Don't pay for him to go to college he's not college material," etc., etc., etc. Mind you, most of the advice was unsolicited, it would come after I would make a comment about something I was planning to do, or just a comment about what was going on in my son's world. As a matter of fact, I became very defensive and after a while, stopped sharing anything with her about my son, because there was never a supporting comment. Instead, there was always a remark about what I doing wrong. One day, I was relating this to one of my friends. She asked me if I had ever asked my mother for advice about raising my son. "After all," she said, "your mother had 4 sons, and had to raise them by herself. She probably feels she is the expert and resents the fact that you never ask for her advice. She most likely feels excluded and instead of saying that to you, expresses it by these criticisms. Why don't you try to ask for her advice once in a while, to see how she responds?"

I decided one day to ask her advice about a sports program he was interested in, and the fact that buying the uniform would be expensive. Much to my surprise, her face lit up. She said "You're asking me for advice?!!" I said, "Yes I really don't know what to do." She started relating stories of my brothers being involved in various sports and how she'd had to struggle to have enough money to buy different kinds of equipment but that it had been worth it. "Janice, yes, let him be involved; you have to sacrifice for your children". I was floored. You mean it was this easy? Now I won't say that I did not still get criticized about different decisions I made, especially if I did not follow her suggestions, but sometimes I would get praise, which had not happened before. My resentment of her criticisms gradually left. My point is that it was all about her feeling excluded, not all about the decisions I had made.

As time passed, and my son became an adult, I no longer sought her advice and the relationship between my mother and I worsened. It had gotten to the point, that every time I visited her, the visit would end with a shouting match. Our relationship had deteriorated to the point where I dreaded being around her. I would be accused of not caring about her feelings, stealing from her, saying things to hurt her, doing things purposely to aggravate her, and putting everyone - my friends, husband and son - before her, and of tricking her into moving out of her house into a Senior Citizens building. To this day, she has not forgiven me.

My brothers and I were really afraid that she would come to harm in her house. There were steep steps going to the upstairs and another flight of stairs going down to the basement. We discovered that she had fallen several times and not told us. The neighborhood was changing and she would forget to set the alarm at night. I took her around to several senior living buildings and she chose one that she liked. She misses her home. She was there for over 30 years, and her reminiscing has turned into feelings that she should have never left. Although her doctor has told her that living there would be dangerous because of her limited mobility and other health issues, she still feels that we tricked her into leaving and says I was the main perpetrator. This was an issue she attacked me with almost every time I would see or talk with her. No matter what I would say, she would end up accusing me of not caring about her feelings.

I live eight miles from her and took her to church every Sunday, went grocery shopping once a week, took her to the doctor every three weeks, ran intermittent errands, helped her around her house and called every other day to make sure that she was alright. But there was one day that impacted me so deeply that I knew something had to give. On this occasion, there were the usual complaints about leaving her house, me caring about her, my smart mouth, etc. Finally I said, "Well, mama, you raised me and people say that I am just like you."

She screamed at me, "You are a damn lie. You're nothing like me, and if anyone else says that, I will tell them to their face that they are a damn lie."

I said, "Well, you are going to be saying that a lot."

That's when she said, "I almost hate you. Get out of my house and never come back." After that incident, I knew something had to change.

I have three living brothers and decided that one of them whom I considered her favorite would have to take over running her errands, taking her to the doctor and taking her to church. This lasted for about a year until he moved out of the state and got married. After he left, he told me all of the disparaging remarks my mother had made about me. He said, "Janice, it's all about her losing control of her life. She is angry because she has lost her independence, her house and her control over her children. Unfortunately, you are the closest to her and she is taking it out on you. You are going to have to deal with it, because you are the only one she can really depend on. Just try to understand."

I began to wonder, am I the only one going through this? Well, that's when I started researching the relationship between adult daughters and their aging mothers. I wanted to have a better understanding of my mother, and at least have a civil relationship with her. I know there are two sides to a story, and wanted to find out what role I played in this relationship. When

I told friends and acquaintances about my idea of writing this book, the responses were overwhelming.

"Oh wow, if you want to interview me, please just call."

"I have so much to say, but you cannot use my name."

"You need to talk to my girlfriend. She is going through hell."

One joked, "I have to take a drink, before and after I visit my mother in order to cope."

These were just a few of the comments. Some people would just start telling me stories about their relationship with their mothers. However, I thought I would start out with my story or stories.

It Wasn't About The Biscuit

We were at a church breakfast and the kitchen had run out of some delicious homemade biscuits. I asked one of the cooks if they were going to have any more available. I was told they would and that they would bring them to the table. I went outside for a while and when I came back, I asked the cook if the biscuits had been brought to the table yet. The cook told me that he had placed it on my brother's plate because the waitstaff had removed my plate. My brother told him that he would give me the biscuit when I returned to the table.

When I returned to the table, I asked my brother for the biscuit. My mother shouted, "NO!!! This is your brother's plate and his biscuit." My brother and I both told her that the cook placed my biscuit on his plate because mine had been removed. My mother again said no emphatically, and then she looked at me and said, "You don't need another biscuit, you've already had two." I said that I had only one biscuit and I wanted another one to take home to my husband. Then Mrs. J, who was sitting next to my mother, said she wanted another biscuit too, since they had cooked more. My mom said, you don't need to wait for them to bring more, and then took a biscuit off of her plate and gave it to Mrs. J.

Mrs. J looked a little puzzled and said, "No, I will wait. You keep the one you are giving me or give it to your daughter."

My mother then said, "No, I don't want that one back, I want the one on my son's plate."

Mrs. J looked even more puzzled, and said, "That's your daughter's. You keep yours, and I can wait."

While this conversation was going on, another cook appeared with a fresh plate of biscuits and stood there with an amused look on his face while this exchange was going on. After a while, he said, "All of this over a biscuit? There are plenty to go around."

Finally, my brother said "mama look, if you want another biscuit, just get one that the cook just brought out. They're nice and warm, and the one on my plate as gotten cold."

My mother looked at him and shouted loudly, "Shut Up!" At this point, my mother had the attention of everyone at the table.

One of the younger ladies whispered to her friend "What's that all about? What's so special about a particular biscuit?"

The next day, my brother told me that he was exasperated and embarrassed by my mother's behavior. He asked her why she was making such a big fuss over a biscuit. My mother told him that it wasn't about the biscuit. She just didn't want me to have it. It was really about my thinking that I could get anything I wanted from anyone and at any time. She felt she had to remind me that everyone was not at my beck and call.

He then asked her, "But, don't you know how that confusion over a biscuit made you look? Everyone could tell it wasn't about the biscuit!"

Her response was, "I don't care. At least I made my point."

Later that same evening, Mrs. J called me. She asked me if there was a problem between me and my mother. She had noticed other instances in church when my mother seemed less than pleased with me, and the biscuit incident seemed over the top. However, she was happy that I responded with patience and not with anger. But I wondered, "Where is all of this coming from?"

Something Has To Change

I am just getting to the point that I am able to write about this without being upset. One day, I was helping my mother take clothes out of some drawers because the exterminator was coming over. There was a problem in her building with pests, and all clothes and bedding had to be removed from her apartment. So far, I had 12 (33 gallon) bags of clothes I had removed. Anyway, I opened one drawer and found her checkbook. Since she is always misplacing stuff, I asked her if she knew that it was in this drawer. Well, that's when it started.

Mama: "Well, I found out that I just can't put my checkbook anyplace," in a very sarcastic manner.

I asked, "What do you mean by that?" She then accused me of writing a $500.00 check without out her permission. I reminded her that I couldn't write a check from her checkbook because she had taken me off of her account. She then told me that it was written to an insurance company. I told her that what she'd received was a letter from the homeowner's insurance company, and if she had read it, it would explain that the money was being withdrawn out of my checking account, but that they'd sent her the letter because she was the owner of the house.

She then accused me (not for the first time) of tricking her into moving out of her house so that I could move my son into her house and move my then boyfriend into my house. She has been living in a senior citizen building for 8 years. My now husband has been living with me for 6 years, including 4 years of marriage. She will not accept that her children were concerned about her safety. Living alone meant dealing with the danger of falling (especially falling down her stairs), the changing neighborhood, and the fact that she would forget to set the alarm, and fall asleep while cooking, etc.

She said I was a liar and a thief! Then I lost it!!!!

I told her I was sick and tired of her accusing me of taking things from her. She denied that she does that. I said perhaps I should have kept a record. I went back over times that she had accused me of taking something, found the stuff, never apologized, and in one incidence, told my brother that she did find a key that I had supposedly stolen, but for him not to tell me that she had found it. Things escalated and I started talking about how she treats me and about how I am the only one who does anything for her.

She said, "You don't have to do anything for me ever."

I said, "I know I don't, but I do things for you because you are my mother and I love you."

She said, "You don't have to love me." Then she called me mean and evil and a liar and thief again, and brought up that when I was a kid, I stole money from her and gave it to my best friend because she was hungry.

I said, "You have been holding this against me for 72 years???!!!" Well I was tired of her treating me like shit. I spelled it out because I've never said a curse word to her. I told her that she treats her sons like kings, even though they do hardly anything for her and don't answer the phone when she calls (which she denied). I reminded her that she tells me that she can't reach them, then I told her that they have caller ID.

She told me to get out and never come back. I said, "I will leave when I am good and ready."

She said, "I will make you leave."

I said, "What are you going to do? Get up and walk over here and push me out of the door?" (I know that was a low blow because she has difficulty walking).

She said, "I can stop you from coming over here."

I said, "Well, if you want to do that, go right ahead."

That's what happened in a nutshell. Afterwards, I was so upset that I sat in my car for over an hour and cried so hard that I hyperventilated. I talked to my brother and a friend of mine who calmed me down.

They both told me that my mother has issues with me and always has had them. It's a matter of jealousy and resentment, possibly because of her anger about her state in life, and she is taking it out on me. They advised me to take a vacation. Be unavailable for a while, to let go of the stress, and make my brother step up.

I knew by that point, she had discovered her mistake, but she hadn't called me. I had most of her clothes at my house because I had to wash them in a commercial laundry, take some to the cleaners, etc.

I decided that I would be unavailable - supposedly out of town. She got the message via a friend of hers. I know all of the dynamics regarding this situation. My grandmother was verbally and physically abusive to her. Although my mother has never been physically abusive, I have had very little validation from her. I love her, but I could not continue to be her whipping post.

I have made sure that she is checked on and that her building staff has my cell and home phone numbers. But for now, I have to regroup and take care of me!

Whew!!! Something has to change.

Perceptions. Who's Right?

Relationships between mothers and daughters can be complicated, especially when the daughter becomes an adult. Some mothers and daughters are best friends. Others talk once a week. Some see each other weekly. Others live far apart. Some have disputes regularly, while others avoid conflict. Some have personal, intimate conversations. Others have superficial conversations. There are ups and downs, no matter how positive (or thorny) the relationship. The emotions revolving around adult daughter and aging mother relationships are often intense and passionate.

Storm clouds in the adult mother-daughter relationship most often arise over one very basic question – will the mother accept the daughter as an adult? That means, when she's visiting you, does she try to run your house? Does she trust you to be independent on small issues as well as large? "Letting the daughter be her own woman is a universal issue," Dr. Tracy explains.

"Mothers and daughters who struggle with their relationships as adults often repeat the old patterns of control and rebellion from childhood", says Dr. Tracy. "They can't hear each other. The daughter will hear the mother say something and she'll think, 'She wants to control me.' And the mother is saying something that absolutely is controlling, but is not meant to be." Meanwhile, when the daughter responds, the mother hears nothing but anger.

What happens that changes this unique parent-child, mother-daughter relationship from a positive one to a negative one? Perceptions!

A sensitive issue between mothers and daughters is giving and receiving criticism. Comments that are perceived as negative about the other's hair, clothes or weight can often lead to conflict. A common complaint among daughters is, "My mother is always critical." At the same time, mothers complain that their daughters take seemingly innocent comments as unintended criticism.

So who's right? It depends on eithers' perception. The mother wants to make suggestions that she feels will improve her daughter's situation. The daughter wants the approval and validation but if it is not what the daughter wants to hear, she often sees it as criticism.

When mothers give their daughters criticism – or vice versa – it's to show how much they care about and love them. "It's a level of attention and focus on detail." Deborah says. "It's a level of scrutiny that you normally reserve for yourself and it can be frustrating when you feel that you're being criticized, but it can be precious when you realize that you could lose it."

"The key to mother-daughter relationships is understanding that there will be mixed feelings and layers of emotions, and different perceptions," Deborah says. For example, as daughters grow up and leave the nest, their mothers often feel both happiness for their success and sadness that they're leaving. "A mother wants her daughter to soar and she's watching her as she soars, but that also means she's receding in the sky," she says. "And so there's that level of feeling loss and left behind at the same time that you feel that pride."

In a study by K. Fingerman, ninety-six older mothers with the average age of 76, and their daughters with the average age of 44 were asked to select the same incident, e.g., a disagreement and rate it individually to the degree that they had engaged in destructive, constructive or avoidant conflict behavior. The mothers claimed they engaged in constructive behavior more than the daughters thought they had. Daughters claimed that they engaged in destructive and avoidant behavior more than their mothers realized. Mothers thought their daughters felt better about the incident than they actually did.

The findings suggested older mothers underestimated their daughter's negative behaviors and feelings about the incident.

A Little More Research

Some studies suggest that almost 30% of women have been alienated from their mothers at some point in their lives. Tension may result from the mother's increasing social selectivity if mothers and daughters perceive the other's behaviors as either demanding of, or inattentive to, their relationship.

The individual descriptions of tension might involve instances where a daughter feels that her mother is meddling or where a mother feels her daughter is excluding her. Yet, the underlying cause of this tension may reflect degrees of investment in the relationship.

Daughters were expected to be more likely to cite their mothers' invasiveness as sources of difficulty, especially when the mothers rated the relationship as most important. Mothers were expected to be more likely to describe feelings of exclusion from their daughters' lives, especially when they were more invested in the relationship.

It is also possible that a mother would consider her own aging as a source of tension with her daughter, particularly if poor health prevented the mother from being involved in the relationship as actively as she had in previous times.

Previously, researchers have found that parents' view of how their grown children turned out has an effect on their own well-being (Ryff, Lee, Essex, & Schmutte, 1994).

Often mothers have issues with the kind of adult their daughters have grown into - especially if the daughter is seen as a somewhat less than an ideal member of society.

"Tell me about the last time you felt irritated, hurt, or annoyed during a visit with your daughter/mother." In the joint interview, mother and daughter had to remember their last tense situation. They were asked to determine the incident that created the last time they had a disagreement or that one of them felt hurt or annoyed by something the other person said or did. The purpose of the joint interview was to have events that both mother and daughter had experienced as tense, to examine how individual perceptions differed from the same experiences. When either one reported that the other did not include her in activities or did not spend enough time with her, it was coded as exclusion.

The majority of mothers spontaneously praised their daughters or commented on positive aspects of their relationship when asked to discuss difficulties. Mothers and daughters alike appeared to consider the other person as important in their lives; the majority of mothers and daughters rated the other person as among the top six most important people in their life. Yet, mothers appeared to give greater positive emotional value to their daughters than daughters did to their mothers. Mothers were more likely to name their daughters as their preferred confidant or the person with whom they most enjoy spending time. Mothers with more children were also more likely to name a child other than the target daughter as their preferred confidant.

Daughters were more likely to find their mothers invasive, and these complaints appear to be related to their mothers' investment in their relationship. Daughters' feelings of being intruded upon were related to their mothers' regarding them as the person they prefer to confide in.

Another important difference in the manner in which mothers and daughters view their relationship appears to be related to how they perceive the boundaries of their relationship. Daughters seem to view their own spouses and offspring as constituting a family unit unto itself, separate from their relationships with their mothers. Daughters also rarely brought up issues involving their mothers in relation to their own spouses, siblings or children. Mothers more often included other people in their discussions of problems with their daughters. Thus, older mothers' investment may lead them to go beyond viewing their daughters as distinct individuals. Rather, mothers may see themselves as an essential part of a larger family, including their daughters, daughters' spouses, siblings, and children. As a result, mothers may feel free to offer advice or to direct matters in their daughters' lives in a manner that daughters find intrusive.

At the same time, mothers seem to experience their daughters' concerns for them as invasive, suggesting that daughters' response to their mothers' aging may be experienced in a negative manner by their mothers, at least when mothers still define themselves as generally healthy.

The pattern of communication between mothers and daughters may be more complex than the portrait presented here, however. The data presented here suggests that mothers and daughters who do not discuss experiences of tension have higher quality relationships. Elsewhere, in findings from the same study of mothers and daughters, I reported that daughters who avoid telling their mothers when they are upset and who have mothers who do not perceive their efforts at avoidance feel worse about the way conflict situations turn out. However, mothers who engaged in aggressive confrontational styles and whose daughters perceive their behaviors as such feel worse about the situation (Fingerman, 1995).

Mothers' focus on other people when discussing what bothered them about their daughters may also have been a means of shielding their daughters from being the sole target of complaint Any daughter who's winced at a mother's criticism won't be surprised to know that mothers continue to mother, and daughters still seek mom's approval late in life. Williamson, now over 50, admits, "I still keep secrets from my mother because there are things about me I don't want her to know."

Can You Relate?

I would like to start with some scenarios I have observed, participated in, or which have been told to me by various adult daughters. I chose these, because after talking with many women, there were several things in common with the incidents and the solutions.

> Patty who is 50 and her mom who is 80 are in the grocery store.
>
> Patty: Did you bring your list?
>
> Mom: I don't need a list, I know what I want. You ask me every time we come to the store, stop asking me that!
>
> Patty: (in an exasperated tone) OK mom, but I just want to make sure you get everything you need, because I am not coming back to the store tomorrow to get something that you have forgotten.
>
> Mom: (in an angry tone) Have I ever asked you to do that?
>
> Patty: Yes
>
> Mom: Well, don't worry, I won't ever ask you to do that again!

Does this sound familiar to you? Maybe not exactly the same, but a similar situation? In other words, can you relate? Here is a technique you can try. Make a list of all of the grocery items your mother uses, food and non-food. Save it to your computer, cell phone, etc. Put it in a table or excel format. Make several copies, and give one to her. Say to her: "I made this list for you to make it easier for you to check off what you need from the store." Call mom before you take her to the store and ask her to go down the list to see what she needs. But, take a copy of the list with you, just in case she doesn't bring the list. When you see something on the list that she does not pick up, as you are going down the aisles, ask, "Do you need_____?"

Now, in the beginning, this might not work, especially if your mom feels that her memory is still good and she doesn't need a list. That's why you still have the list with you. But you must be patient, because over time, she will begin to appreciate it. As a matter of fact, one woman told me that her mother "forgot" her list, and in the store said, "Well, where is your list? You must always bring your list, just in case I forget mine again." Her daughter smiled to herself and thought "victory"! Their trips to the grocery store are much more pleasant now.

Let's look at another scenario. Donna is 42 and her mother is 66. Due to health problems, her mother has limited mobility and has to use a walker. When Donna and her mother were younger, they would go shopping at the malls and department stores on a regular basis together. As mom became older and less mobile, the shopping trips became tiring and less enjoyable to her, however, she still insisted on going. Donna decided she would take her mother to one large department store, and when her mother became tired, she would search out items for her mother, and take them to her while her mother sat on her walker and rested. After a while, Donna stopped taking her mom because she could see that it was too much of a strain on her mother. She started going shopping without her mother and when she would see items she thought her mother would like, she would purchase them. As time went by, mom didn't like anything that Donna bought her and started saying, "I know why you don't take me to the store anymore. You don't want to be bothered with me. I'm just too much trouble. I'm going to go by myself like I used to. I'm going to catch the bus and go shopping without you."

When Donna tried to explain to her mother that she was trying to make it easier for her, her mother wouldn't accept it, and became even angrier. As a result, Donna started feeling unappreciated, hurt and angry. This went on for a while until Donna exploded one day and said "How are you going to catch a bus and you can't even step up on a curb without help? You go on and catch that bus, but don't call me when you are in trouble!"

Mom said "I will, and don't worry I won't call you, and don't buy me anything else. I can buy my own clothes." One day, Donna overheard her mother telling one of her friends, "I would like to buy a new sweater, but my daughter won't take me shopping anymore. I guess I'll try to go by myself." For days after that, when Donna and her mother were together, the relationship was strained.

Donna was afraid her mother would actually do it, and her mother was angry because of what Donna said. Does this sound a little familiar to you? Maybe not the exact situation, but a similar one. Can you relate?

Here is a technique you can try. Do you have a laptop, IPad, or is there a computer available for your mother to look at? Even though her mother had purchased from QVC and HSN, Donna decided to introduce her mother to online shopping. She searched out her mom's favorite stores and demonstrated how they could still shop together while on the computer. Her mother was amazed that she could look at as many items as she wanted, and enjoyed choosing an item, ordering it, and receiving it in the mail. Now every other Sunday afternoon, Donna and her mother go on their "virtual" shopping trips together. Mom has what she wants - together time shopping with her daughter and Donna has what she missed - a pleasant shopping trip with her mother.

Lisa is 51 and her mother is 75. When Lisa was in her early 20's and 30's and single, she and her mother would travel together. They have visited foreign countries and gone on several cruises and weekend trips. As Lisa grew into her 40's, she began to travel with some of her friends but would include her mother on these trips. Although Lisa and her friends enjoyed her mother's company, they began to feel that she was orchestrating their activities according to what she liked, and would criticize them when they wanted to do something different. Case in point: On a trip to Italy, Lisa and her girlfriend decided to go out late one night to a club. Her mother, became angry and said, "You just don't want to include me. You probably didn't want me to come, anyway. Tomorrow we are going on a tour early in the morning. I suggest you should stay in and go to bed early so you will be ready for the tour the next morning." Of course, Lisa and her friend went anyway. The next morning at breakfast, she wouldn't speak to them. A couple of days later, Lisa's mother was exhausted because of the all of the walking in the heat and decided to take a nap. So Lisa decided that she and her friend would go shopping while her mother slept. When they returned, her mother complained bitterly, and said "So, you sneaked out and left me again. You should not have gone. You keep intentionally leaving me out. Why don't you just tell me I'm too old and you wish I had never come? I will never travel with you again."

On the last day of the trip, the tour group was to view the Trevi Fountain. The tour guide pulled Lisa aside and said that because the temperature was 102 degrees and they would have to walk a distance to get to the fountain, he felt that it would be too much for her mother because he noticed that she seemed exhausted and her legs and feet were swollen. He preferred that she remain on the air conditioned bus with the driver until they returned. Her mother, protesting vehemently, felt that Lisa just didn't want her along and no amount of explaining could calm her down. Lisa decided to remain on the bus with her mother to prove that she had not orchestrated this. The atmosphere for the rest of the trip was strained and unpleasant.

When they arrived home, Lisa overheard her mother telling her friend how she was left behind several times, didn't enjoy the trip, and Lisa was selfish. Of course, Lisa felt hurt and decided she would no longer include her mother in her travel plans. Lisa would travel, not tell her mother, or tell her afterwards. As time went on, her mother was more resentful, and the relationship was more strained.

Well, does this sound familiar to you, maybe not the exact scenario, but a similar situation? In other words, can you relate?

I told Lisa that when she excluded her mother from all of her travel plans, essentially, she was getting back at her mother for the spoiled trip and for the words she heard her mother say. The result of her actions was causing the strained relationship and she was being immature. Since traveling together was a large part of their relationship, her mother felt abandoned. I suggested to Lisa that instead of excluding her mother from traveling with her, she should plan at least one major trip a year for just she and her mother and her focus would be that this trip was for her mother's enjoyment. In other words, whatever her mother wanted to do, do it! Her mother always talked about going to the Grand Canyon, so Lisa planned a trip for them in the spring and in the late summer, Lisa took her on a weekend trip. When Lisa told her mother that she and some her friends were going on a cruise at the end of the year, Lisa waited for the explosion. Instead, her mother said, "That sounds really nice, I hope you and your friends have a wonderful time, just bring me back a souvenir."

What's Wrong With The Way I Dress???!!!

Amy is 70 years old, but she is usually mistaken for a woman in her early 40's. She works out regularly, has a slim figure, is very attractive and has a pleasant, outgoing personality. She shops where young women shop and chooses clothes, shoes, and other accessories that are youthful. Although she has a little grey hair, she chooses to color it and her hair styles are contemporary. She often changes her hairstyle and color from long to short or from brunette to blond. She is often complimented on her choice of clothes, accessories, and hairstyles.

Her mother often criticizes the way she dresses and the way she styles her hair. Here are some examples. "You are 70 years old, you should dress your age, and why don't you just let your hair go grey? Where did you get that lipstick? It's hideous. Every time I see you, you have a new pair of shoes, why don't you just buy some basic pumps and stop wearing all of those different styles? You shop too much." These conversations usually end with Amy becoming angry. One day she told me that she hates to wear anything new if she is going to be with her mother and often finds herself not wanting to be with her mother. One day she told her mother that she is sick and tired of her criticizing the way she looks and would appreciate it if she would just not make a comment at all.

Her mother agreed, but Amy said, "Now when I see her, she just gives me that look." One Sunday at church, a young man complimented Amy's mother on the dress she was wearing. He said, "Wow, you look so pretty in that dress. You look better than your daughter."

Her mother commented, "Well, I can understand that!" Later her mother told her that that young man's comment proved that she was right about the way Amy dressed, and that she should change. Amy reminded her that she had bought that dress for her, and instead of looking in the "Old Ladies Department", which would have been more appropriate, she decided to buy her something fashionable instead of some more of those frumpy clothes that she insisted on wearing. Her mother looked hurt and refused to speak to Amy for the rest of the day.

On another occasion, Amy took her mother to the hair salon. Amy's hair had been dyed red. When she and her mother entered the salon, the beauticians complimented her and told her that she was looking younger every day. One of the trainee beauticians wanted to know the name of the colorist she went to, because her next training was to include coloring hair. While all of this was going on, Amy looked at her mother who was sitting with a scowl on her face. One of the older beauticians made the mistake of asking Amy's mother how she liked her hair. Amy's mother replied, "She looks like a whore." The shop got instantly quiet.

Amy looked at her mother and said, "At least, I still have hair to color," and stormed out. Amy asked me, "What should I do? This is frustrating and I really didn't mean to be sarcastic and hurt her feelings, but I can't stand her negative remarks."

As I have said, I don't have all of the answers. Maybe my readers can blog me to give Amy some suggestions.

Yo' Mama

Do you know what kind of childhood your mother had or what kind of relationship she had with her mother? Often the relationships our mothers have with us are patterned after their own mother daughter relationship. But also, the opposite can be true. That mother daughter relationship may have been so contentious or negative that the mother might decide to make sure that her relationship with her daughter is just the opposite. I have two examples that show how the previous mother daughter relationship directly impacted the present relationship.

As Linda was growing up, her mother was a strict disciplinarian, very controlling and often used corporal punishment. Sometimes the punishment was severe enough to cause bruising. Linda's mother and father would often fight verbally and physically about disciplining Linda. When Linda was in her teens, her mother would not let her be involved in any social activities and did not let her date. She often disapproved of any girlfriends Linda had. Her parents divorced while Linda was in her teens. When Linda became a young adult, she got a job and moved from her mother's home. Of course, as Linda says, she "let loose". "It was so great not to be under my mother's thumb, that I went wild." She became promiscuous and irresponsible and became estranged from her mother. But as she got older, she calmed down, finished college and embarked on a very successful career. She decided that she wanted to renew her relationship with her mother and reached out to her. In the beginning things were wonderful and she and her mother got along very well.

When Linda decided to get married, she introduced her fiancé to her mother and as Linda says, "things began to breakdown." Her mother began to criticize Linda's girlfriends and her fiancé and began to criticize Linda's every decision regarding her job, her girlfriends and her fiancé. She would often tell Linda not to trust her fiancé because he was probably seeing other women. As Linda said, "My old mother returned. Even to the point that she became so angry with me on one occasion (because I did not do what she thought I should have done), that she slapped me. It felt to me that I was back in the relationship that I had with my mother when I was a child."

When Linda got married, her mother refused to come to the wedding. As time went by, Linda had two children. When she invited her mother to both christenings, her mother refused to attend because, as she said, "You aren't going to raise them right, anyway."

"I just don't understand my mother! Why is she like this?" As she related all of this to me, I asked Linda if she knew anything about how her mother was raised. She said that she only knew that her mother and grandmother did not get along, but had never really thought too much about it. I told her maybe she should find out why her mother and grandmother don't get along. A couple of months later, Linda called me and related to me what her mother finally told her about her grandmother.

It seems as though her mother was raised in an abusive home. She was the youngest and often received the brunt of her mother's anger. Her mother told her she was an accident and was going to grow up to be nothing. She was either verbally or physically abused on a daily basis until she ran away from home when she was a teenager. She married an older man who also physically abused her and was unfaithful. Eventually she met and married Linda's father. Linda said that she now understood why her mother acted the way she did. "It's like she is reliving her life through me." Linda thinks that her mother, in her own way, is trying to protect her from the life she led. "Since my mother told me about her life, it seems to have opened the door to more communication. When she slips into relating to me like her mother related to her, I gently remind her that I love her, and understand why she is saying the things she says. I also have told her why I left home so soon and acted out in the ways that I did. We are both working towards an understanding of each other. We still have some ways to go, but our relationship is much better."

The Letter

Dear Mama,

It took me a while to write you this letter because I wanted to choose my words wisely.

It seems to me as though our mother-daughter relationship is deteriorating into a very unpleasant relationship. The last time I was at your apartment, we had a terrible argument which affected me very deeply. I sat in your parking lot for over an hour because I was too upset to drive. This was the first time that I cried so hard that I hyperventilated.

I realize that you are unhappy where you are and that you miss your house. But I did not trick you into moving. You said that I wanted you out of your house so that Shaun could move there and Sam could move in with me. I had no plans for Sam to live with me. He had his own apartment in Aurora. Sam did not move in with me until he started getting Cancer treatment, which was over a year after you moved. It would not have mattered to me whether Shaun was here or not.

But what I really wanted to talk about is how much you hurt me. You accused me of writing a $500.00 check from your checking account, which is impossible for me to do because you took me off of your account. I tried to explain to you that the letter you received from the insurance company was a confirmation of the payments that come out of MY checking account. You called me mean, evil, a liar and a thief and brought up something that I did when I was a kid. I never knew that you still held things against me from over 50-60 years ago. You even told me to get out of your house and never come back, and that you could stop me from coming over there. When I told you that I do things for you because I love you, you said I didn't have to love you. You made me feel like I was a stranger – somebody off of the streets, the words you said to me and the way you looked at me hurt me to the core.

Then at the Church breakfast, you made a big deal over my having a biscuit, and told Bob that you just didn't want me to have it. To top all of this off, you told my brother that I must be having problems at home and must have a drinking problem. Then I find out that you talk negatively to Thelma, the manager of your building, about me. Don't get angry at her, because she wasn't the one who told me. So I started thinking, if you talk to her about me, who else thinks I am a horrible person? Do you remember how you felt when your mother would talk about you to other people making you out to be a not-so-nice person and you were doing all you could for her? I feel the same way.

When we are together, it's very seldom pleasant. I said to you that when you see me you don't smile, and it's the truth. I feel that you are much happier when my brother Frank, Robert or even your granddaughter are around you, or do most things for you instead of me. In essence, I feel tolerated. Whenever anyone says we are alike, you vehemently deny it. How do you think that makes me feel? I am proud when people say you're just like your mother. You once told me in a fit of anger that you almost hate me, so maybe that's why you say that I am nothing like you.

I went out of town, but for only three days. I have been home for a while, finishing up your clothes. I haven't called you because every time I think about that day, I still feel like crying. I am sorry that we don't have the kind of mother-daughter relationship that's pleasant for both of us. Maybe one day we can have an honest, open conversation, and really listen to one another without anger. But I still love you, even though I don't have to.

A few days later, I asked my mother if she had read the letter. She said that she had and threw it away. When I asked her why, she became belligerent and said, "Was I supposed to keep it? I threw it away because there was nothing in it. You have told me these things before." I then said that maybe we could talk about my feelings. She said that it was unnecessary and maybe we should talk about HER feelings.

So What About Her Feelings?

Let's talk about your mother's feelings, and why she feels and/or acts the way she does. Is she responding to the way you communicate with her? How do you show your appreciation? Have you ever told her you appreciate her? Do you approach your relationship with your mother as far as who is right and who is wrong? Have you tried to figure her out? Do you make her feel valuable? What kind of language do you use?

Give her what you want her to give back to you. If your mother dies, and you don't attempt it, your pain will be much greater. Maybe she does not have good skills for love. Look at her past. How was she raised? Maybe she is being the best mother she can be using the tools that she has. Mothers and daughters have a bond that no one else shares. Don't overlook her feelings. Spending time with her says to her that she matters. Is the little girl in you getting in the way of reconciling with your mother?

In T.D. Jakes video entitled, Mother and Daughter at War, he gives three steps to healing a broken mother and daughter relationship.

1. Acknowledge the other person's pain, don't defend yourself. Their pain is real, feel it with them so that they are not alone, because lonely people get angry.

2. Apologize for your part in it. Don't defend it don't excuse it.

3. Be consistently connected to what happened. Live in the moment, not in the past, not in the future, step into the moment even when the moment is ugly, because they want you there, good or bad, right or wrong. They want you present in the moment. You can be physically present but still emotionally abandoning them.

Shirley shared this with me about a conversation with her mother:

"One Mother's Day, I was sitting with my mother. Not for the first time, I asked her to tell me about my deceased grandmother. Usually, when I would ask her about her childhood, and the relationship she had with my grandmother, she would say it was just a regular childhood. But on this day, she started telling me about her childhood.

Her mother was absent most of the time because she was a party girl. From late Thursday night to Sunday night, her mother would spend hours away at local bars, dance halls and various parties. Although she did not work during the week, she was often tired and too sleepy to give my mother much time. 'My mother was a good student,' Shirley said, 'and when she would bring home excellent grades from school, my grandmother would barely acknowledge them.' She said that she often felt abandoned and lonely.

When she decided to leave home at 17, my grandmother said, 'Well, it's about time.' When my grandmother became ill, my mother moved back home to take care of her. My mother said that's when my grandmother would apologize to her about not being the kind of mother she should have been and would ask her over and over to please forgive her."

Then her mother said something that opened Shirley's eyes. She said, "I guess that's why I hold on to you so very hard, forget that you are grown and can make your own decisions. And I guess that's why we often argue, and I don't hear from you a lot. Sometimes, I feel like you are abandoning me, and I don't want that." Wow!

How Your Behavior Affects Her Behavior: A Psychological Explanation

There are two types of behavior reinforcements - positive and negative. When thinking about reinforcement, always remember that the end result is to try to increase or decrease a particular behavior.

Positive reinforcement is the way by which behavior is increased. Positive reinforcement works by presenting a motivating incentive to the person after the desired behavior is displayed. In other words, it's adding something positive in order to increase a response.

Negative reinforcement happens when a certain incentive is removed after a particular behavior is displayed. The likelihood of the particular behavior occurring again in the future is increased because of the removal of the negative consequence. In other words, taking away something in order to increase a behavior that you want to see. Negative reinforcement should not be thought of as a punishment. With negative reinforcement, you are increasing a behavior, whereas with punishment, you are decreasing a behavior.

I thought I would expand on the definition of negative reinforcement, which can sometimes be confusing. Whatever reinforcement you use, it needs to be immediate, consistent, and powerful enough to motivate. Basically all you are doing is rewarding the desired behavior

So what does this have to do with you and your relationship with your mother? How are you behaving towards your mother, both consciously and unconsciously? How does this effect the way she behaves towards you? The process of changing behavior starts by identifying a behavior you want to increase and the circumstances around it. Pick your target behavior and notice what happens before and after. What behavior do you see in yourself and in your mother that you want to change? Let's look at some examples of both positive and negative reinforcement behavior that can change both your and your mother's responses.

Positive Reinforcement

You give your mother a big smile and hug (positive reinforcement) for buying you something nice (behavior). You give your mother praise (positive reinforcement) when she takes her medicine as the doctor ordered (behavior). You compliment your mother (positive reinforcement) when she smiles (behavior). What are some behaviors in yourself and your mother that you want to increase? For example, telling your mother that you enjoy (positive reinforcement) your heart to heart talks (behavior).

Negative Reinforcement

For negative reinforcement, think of it as taking something negative away in order to increase a positive behavior.

Punishment

When people hear punishment, they typically think of a negative or harmful consequence. However, this is not always the case. Punishment is usually used to decrease unwanted behavior.

There are two types of punishment - positive and negative, and it can be difficult to tell the difference between the two. Below are some examples to help clear up the confusion.

What is Positive Punishment?

Positive punishment works by presenting a negative consequence after an undesired behavior is exhibited, making the behavior less likely to happen in the future. The following are some examples of positive punishment:

Let's look at some examples of both positive and negative punishing behavior that can change both your and your mother's responses.

You stop talking to your mother (negative consequence) when she criticizes your choice in friends (undesired behavior). Your mother criticizes the way you dress (negative consequence) when you criticize the way she dresses (undesired behavior).

What is Negative Punishment? Negative punishment happens when a certain desired stimulus or motivation is removed after a particular undesired behavior is exhibited, resulting in the behavior happening less often in the future.

Example: You stop cooking your mother's favorite dish (desired stimulus) when she doesn't take her medications (undesired behavior). With punishment, always remember that the end result is to try to decrease the undesired behavior. Positive punishment involves adding a negative consequence after an undesired behavior to decrease future responses. Negative punishment includes taking away a certain desired item after the undesired behavior happens in order to decrease future instances of negative behavior.

It should be noted that research shows that positive consequences are more powerful than negative consequences for improving behavior. However, in my opinion, punishment should never be used whether it is considered negative or positive when you are changing adult behavior. I included the definition of punishment to make you more self-aware of the type of behavior you and your mother may be exhibiting.

From Negative To Positive

We all have to deal with difficult people at some point in our lives, but what can be the most challenging is learning how to deal with negative energy from one of our closest family members.

At times, it may not be easy to achieve a balance between a sense of compassion without being dragged into their negativity, which is why I'd like to share with you five simple tips for dealing with a negative family member.

Tip 1. Accept Them For Who They Are

It may not be easy to offer compassion to someone you feel resentment towards, but trying to understand their feelings and ultimately accepting them for who they are, will help you feel better when you're around them.

Tip 2. Create Positive Boundaries

Make sure you're giving them enough space and that you set your own boundaries by staying positive or neutral. Visualizing a protective energy around yourself will also help you feel stronger, if you can't put distance between yourself and your family member.

Tip 3. Be Aware Of Your Need To Control

You can't control other people's negativity or opinions, so resist the urge to argue if your family member triggers a negative energy inside of you. Your job is not to fix everyone's problems, so instead of being a part of the problem by feeding it with more emotions, disengage by remaining calm and letting yourself be a witness, not a participant.

Tip 4. Learn From Them

There's always something to learn from any situation, and negative family members can be great spiritual teachers as they can help to show you what you're holding on to. Don't waste the opportunity to learn from these situations.

Tip 5. Nurture Yourself

This may be the most important tip of all. Remember that by nurturing yourself and your self-confidence, YOU will become stronger!

Tap into your compassion to find inner peace and don't forget to foster the relationships that lift you up and bring you the most happiness in your life!

Natalie ~ Mind Movies

Meetings Can Lead To Resolutions

I have related a few scenarios that I have been given since I started talking about this book. While I was doing some research, I came across some suggestions from Dr. Venus E. Evans-Winters, a Contributing Writer for Everyday Feminism and an Associate Professor of Education and Faculty Affiliate of Women and Gender Studies. Here are some excerpts that, hopefully, will be of help to you with resolving some of the issues relating to difficult mother/daughter relationships.

Step 1: Set Up The Meeting

Set up a get-together with your mother in advance. Let her choose a time and date to meet. Inform your mother in advance what the meeting will be about. Decide if it will take place in a private place, like your living room, or in a public place. Weigh the pros and cons of a public versus private meeting.

Also, you should know in advance what it is you want to say to your mother and the message you would like to express. Do not have any other family members at the meeting. The point is to avoid family members siding with or teaming up against mother or daughter.

After the initial reconciliation talk, other family members can come together and discuss the renewal of the relationship or how to help support the relationship.

Step 2: Have the Conversation

Begin the conversation by thanking your mother for agreeing to join you in the conversation. Let her know that the meeting is very important to you. Then, start the conversation talking about the positive aspects of your relationship. If there is no relationship at all at this point, you can simply begin by pointing out positive characteristics of your mother or positive events or behaviors in her past.

Most importantly, instead of beginning the conversation with whom or what caused the problem, begin with pointing out strengths about the person or the relationship. Be specific about the behavior or characteristic that you feel attracts you (or others) to your mother, that makes you appreciate and value her as a human being, and makes you want to be near her more often.

Both of you should be given the chance to identify strengths about the relationship before discussing the undesirable aspects of the relationship. It may be difficult to identify strengths, especially when someone has been in pain for a long time. However, it is very important to let your mother know that she is not a bad person in your eyes. Focus on characteristics that draw you to her. No one wants to be criticized by someone they love.

Step 2a: O.P.E.N. Up My Heart, My Mouth, & My Ears

To make this step easier, Dr. Winters derived the acronym: OPEN. Think of this step in the healing talk as "OPEN" up my heart, my mouth, and my ears.

(O)wn

"It is important during the initial dialogue that you own up to your part of the discord. Explain to your mother what mistakes you have made in the past and how you may have contributed to the negative dynamics of the relationship.

(P)inpoint

In this stage of the discussion, pinpoint specifically the action or event that caused you to withdraw from the relationship or lose trust in your parent. In other words, be specific in naming exactly what behavior or set of behaviors hurt you. Sometimes individuals in families are vague in stating the true problem; therefore, it is difficult to avoid correcting the problem. Consequently, the unwanted behavior is never changed.

(E)go

For me, this is the most important step in any meaningful discussion. Simply stated, suspend your ego. Now is not the time to be concerned with winning an argument. Even more important, do not worry about being embarrassed or appearing emotionally weak. The goal is not to win an argument or to save face, but to amend a very important relationship.

(N)ext

Where do you want to go from here? In other words, what do you hope to accomplish from the discussion or what do you expect now from you, your mother and your mother-daughter relationship?"

Step 3: Move Forward

Move forward from the struggle toward healing. Dr. Winters suggests that you plan to spend some short time alone together with your mother. Set up a brief outing, e.g., lunch, dinner, or a movie. After a few brief outings, then you and your mother can work on spending longer times together.

Here is a suggestion from Margarita Tartakovsky, M.S. who is an Associate Editor at Psych Central. Make the first move. Even though you feel that you are in the right and your mother is definitely wrong, make the first move to change yourself. Have realistic expectations. Communicate. Be an active listener. Repair damage quickly. Put yourself in her shoes. Learn to forgive. Balance individuality and closeness. Agree to disagree. Stick to the present. "Use 'I' statements, rather than being accusatory," Cohen-Sandler said. Set boundaries. Don't bring in third parties."

I Can See Clearly

Have you ever heard of visualization? I have and when I first heard about it, I thought, yeah right! I have visualized a lot of things that have not come to pass. I did not know that there is definitely a process to go through. I have found it has helped me in many situations and especially in the relationship with my mother. I'm going to give you some steps that I found by reading a book called, The Gateway, by Robert Sidell. He gives six steps of what he calls empowered visualization. The steps involve using multisensory visualization. He suggests that you write a script of how you would like an experience to be.

Using Vivid Multisensory Images

My script was as follows. I go to visit my mother in her apartment. When she opens the door, I smile. I smell something cooking. I give her a hug and feel the texture of her skin, the texture of her favorite robe that she is always wearing. I have a feeling of happiness that I am in her presence. We have a very pleasant conversation on a subject matter that I know will not cause an argument. When she says something that would usually cause me to bristle, I smile and know that this is going to be a pleasant visit.

See Related Consequences of Attaining Your Goal

Because my goal was to have a pleasant relationship with my mother, I imagined my related consequences to be having good positive conversations, seeing her laughing and enjoying my company, going shopping together, going to movies together again, and feeling a sense of peace in her and myself when we are in each other's presence. I kept visualizing these things to make them real in my mind.

Involve Others In Your Imagery

Since my husband, brother and close friends knew about the difficulty I was having in my relationship with my mother, I asked them to help me by visualizing positive interactions. When

I would be in my mother's company, either visiting her in her apartment, taking her to the store, or taking her to the doctor, I would tell them exactly what we would be doing and asked them to visualize us having a very pleasant time. Afterwards I would tell them about our visits whether they were good or bad. If it was an unpleasant visit, I would ask them to visualize and to pray!

Speak About Your Dream/Goal As If It Has Already Happened

I started doing a lot of self-talk. I also would talk with my husband in positive terms about my relationship with my mother. The more my talk was positive; it seemed that things were indeed changing for the best.

Take Action

Of course, you can visualize all you want, but if you don't take any action, whatever your goal or dream is probably will not come to past. Your subconscious is a powerful thing and when you bring your subconscious thoughts into action, amazing things can happen.

Ask For Divine Guidance For Your Dream/Goal

In the end, ask God to guide you. Even better, ask him in the beginning!

Save Yourself

Trying to have a better relationship with your mother can be stressful. You must remember that in order to be there for you and your mother, you have to be able to deal with all of the emotions that this relationship brings about. Here are some ways in which you can relieve stress.

Just a note – I would go get a regular checkup and my blood pressure was always normal. But when I would take my mother, the doctor would check my blood pressure along with hers. My mother's was normal (she is on blood pressure medication), so it is regulated by the medication. Mine was usually high on these visits. The doctor would look at me and say, "Well, I can understand why it is high today, but you must know how to save yourself. I am going to offer you some ways in which you can relieve stress." I have found that numbers 1, 2, 8 and 9, really work for me. Choose what you think will work for you and by all means stick to it! You can find these techniques on WebMD.

Relaxation Techniques That Zap Stress Fast
By Jeannette Moninger
WebMD Feature
Reviewed by Michael W. Smith, MD
Each of these stress-relieving tips takes less than 15 minutes.
1. Meditate
A few minutes of practice per day can help ease anxiety. "Research suggests that daily meditation may alter the brain's neural pathways, making you more resilient to stress," says psychologist Robbie Maller Hartman, PhD, a Chicago health and wellness coach. It's simple. Sit up straight with both feet on the floor. Close your eyes. Focus your attention on reciting -- out loud or silently -- a positive mantra such as "I feel at peace" or "I love myself." Place one hand on your belly to sync the mantra

with your breaths. Let any distracting thoughts float by like clouds.

2. Breathe Deeply

Take a 5-minute break and focus on your breathing. Sit up straight, eyes closed, with a hand on your belly. Slowly inhale through your nose, feeling the breath start in your abdomen and work its way to the top of your head. Reverse the process as you exhale through your mouth. "Deep breathing counters the effects of stress by slowing the heart rate and lowering blood pressure," psychologist Judith Tutin, PhD, says. She's a certified life coach in Rome, GA.

3. Be Present

Slow down. "Take 5 minutes and focus on only one behavior with awareness," Tutin says. Notice how the air feels on your face when you're walking and how your feet feel hitting the ground. Enjoy the texture and taste of each bite of food. When you spend time in the moment and focus on your senses, you should feel less tense.

4. Reach Out

Your social network is one of your best tools for handling stress. Talk to others -- preferably face to face, or at least on the phone. Share what's going on. You can get a fresh perspective while keeping your connection strong.

5. Tune In to Your Body

Mentally scan your body to get a sense of how stress affects it each day. Lie on your back, or sit with your feet on the floor. Start at your toes and work your way up to your scalp, noticing how your body feels. "Simply be aware of places you feel tight or loose without trying to change anything," Tutin says. For 1 to 2 minutes, imagine each deep breath flowing to that body part. Repeat this process as you move your focus up your body, paying close attention to sensations you feel in each body part.

6. Decompress

Place a warm heat wrap around your neck and shoulders for 10 minutes. Close your eyes and relax your face, neck, upper chest, and back muscles. Remove the wrap, and use a tennis ball or foam roller to massage away tension. "Place the ball between your back and the wall. Lean into the ball, and hold gentle pressure for up to 15 seconds. Then move the ball to another spot, and apply pressure," says Cathy Benninger, a nurse practitioner and assistant professor at The Ohio State University Wexner Medical Center in Columbus.

7. Laugh Out Loud

A good belly laugh doesn't just lighten the load mentally. It lowers cortisol, your body's stress hormone, and boosts brain chemicals called endorphins, which help your mood. Lighten up by tuning in to your favorite sitcom or video, reading the comics, or chatting with someone who makes you smile.

8. Crank Up the Tunes

Research shows that listening to soothing music can lower blood pressure, heart rate, and anxiety. "Create a playlist of songs or nature sounds (the ocean, a bubbling brook, birds chirping), and allow your mind to focus on the different melodies, instruments, or singers in the piece," Benninger says. You also can blow off steam by rocking out to more upbeat tunes -- or singing at the top of your lungs!

9. Get Moving

You don't have to run in order to get a runner's high. All forms of exercise, including yoga and walking, can ease depression and anxiety by helping the brain release feel-good chemicals and by giving your body a chance to practice dealing with stress. You can go for a quick walk around the block, take the stairs up and down a few flights, or do some stretching exercises like head rolls and shoulder shrugs.

10. Be Grateful

Keep a gratitude journal or several (one by your bed, one in your purse, and one at work) to help you remember all the things that are good in your life. "Being grateful for your blessings cancels out negative thoughts and worries," says Joni Emmerling, a wellness coach in Greenville, NC. Use these journals to savor good experiences like a child's smile, a sunshine-filled day, and good health. Don't forget to celebrate accomplishments like mastering a new task at work or a new hobby. When you start feeling stressed, spend a few minutes looking through your notes to remind yourself what really matters.

The Little Bell

Often I would sit with various friends and colleagues and talk about this book and they would regale me with funny stories.

Tina: My mother has always loved to collect bells. When she came to live with me, I gave her one of her favorite crystal bells to ring when she needed me. What did I do that for? The beautiful sound that comes from a crystal bell ringing began to sound like a gong! How can you ring a bell 12 times in a 5 minute period? Ting a ling, just wanted to make sure you cook my eggs over easy. Ting a ling, make sure the bacon doesn't burn. Ting a ling, is the water boiling for my coffee? Ting a ling, don't forget the toast. Ting a ling, ting a ling... The last ting a ling was "Just wanted to make sure you could hear the bell". That night when she was asleep, I took the bell. The next morning, I told her it was so beautiful, I didn't want her to break it.

Lilly: I go to the gym 3 days a week and leave my cell phone in my purse while I am exercising so that I won't be disturbed. One day, when I finished and looked at my cell phone, there were several calls from my daughter. I called her back and she said, "Mama you have got to come home right now, right away. The police have been here twice!!!" I was very alarmed because my mother lives with us.

"What's wrong??!!!"

She said, "The alarm keeps going off and when we shut it off, it goes off again. We called the alarm company and they said that there is nothing wrong, something in the house is setting off the alarm." When I got home, the alarm was sounding, I turned it off, and a few minutes later it sounded again. I looked for the remote and could not find it. Then the alarm sounded again. There was a banging at the door, and there were the police again. We asked my mother if she knew where the remote was. Now she is in the early stages of dementia and could only remember that she saw it in her bedroom. So we searched and searched and still could not find it. The alarm sounded again, we began to notice that every time my mother moved, the alarm would go off. She had on her robe so we looked in her pockets, but could not find it. She sat down in her favorite chair and kicked off her house shoes, the alarm went off. Well, we found the alarm. It was in the toe of one of her house shoes, and every time she moved the alarm sounded!

The policeman and I both laughed so hard tears were running down our faces! My mother has neuropathy in her toes and could not feel the alarm. When I called the alarm company to tell them what was happening, the representative laughed and said, "This is the first time I have heard this one!" Fortunately he decided not to charge us extra for all of the false alarms.

June: I take my 88-year-old mother to the doctor to get her checkups. When we scheduled her next appointment, the doctor said that she would not be available therefore the nurse would see her and she would peek in just to say hello to see how she was doing. Well, when the nurse finished she went to get the doctor. The doctor came in, sat down, and she was a little upset because my mother had not been taking her medication as prescribed. When the doctor asked her why she wasn't taking the medication (a diuretic), my mother replied, "Because I have to go to the bathroom too much. And besides, I thought you said you would just peek in."

The doctor said, "I am."

My mother said, "No, you are all the way in."

The doctor just smiled and said, "Well, I'll be more specific next time."

My mother said, "Right. You are a doctor and I know you have an extensive vocabulary, use the correct words next time."

The doctor said, "Mrs. S, I would not have come in if you had been taking your medication properly."

My mother said, with a grin, "Are you sassing me young lady?"

The doctor said, with a bigger grin, "No, ma'am. Boy, you remind me of my mother." They both laughed.

Gale: Sometimes I think I need a long straw to put in my favorite bottle of wine.

Rita: I have a small bottle of liquor on my mother's back porch. From time to time, I have to go and get me a little sip.

Anne: My mother told me that her neighbor across the hall wanted to know why when I leave her apartment, they would hear a loud sigh!

Sharon: My mother and I were in Europe. I went into the bathroom and shouted, "Mama, we have a bidet!"

My mother said, "What are you shouting about? Of course, we have a BIG DAY."

"No mama, you must come in and see it."

"How am I going to see a big day from the bathroom?"

"Please, mama, come into the bathroom."

As she was coming into the bathroom, she said "Is there a list of things to do in the bathroom? You could have just brought it out for me to see." I pointed to the bidet. Mama said "Well why you didn't say so!"

Maria: I bought my mom a laptop computer to keep her busy. I wondered why she waited until late at night to be on it. One night, around 1:00 a.m., I heard her giggling. When I went into her bedroom, she was on the computer. I asked her what was so funny. She said, "My boyfriend just told me a funny joke."

"Your boyfriend?!"

"Yes, we talk around this time every night because of the time difference. He's in Europe."

I asked her if her boyfriend knew that she was 80 years old. She said, "He likes older women." I reminded her of men who are on the computer and ask for money. She said "Do you think I'm stupid? I won't give your no-account brother money. What makes you think I would give a man who I don't even know money? If he dares ask me for money, I'll just find another boyfriend! Now go back to bed, and let me enjoy myself."

Sandra: One evening, I walked into my parents' house without ringing the bell first. There were my mother and father on the couch doing some heavy petting (they are both in their early 80's). My mother said, "Don't you know how to knock before you come in?" I told her that I didn't expect to see them doing THAT. She said "How do you think you got here - by Immaculate Conception?"

Reflections

You know there are some things you remember vividly from your childhood that for some reason stay with you. I remember sitting on the porch after my mother washed my hair. My hair was very long and thick and tangled easily. She would sit in a chair and I would sit in between her legs while she combed, brushed and braided my hair. I was what they called "tender headed". Every comb out would make me cringe. She would say, "It hurts now but you will look so pretty when I finish." And I did.

Every winter morning she would line my brothers and me up and give us a tablespoon of cod liver oil and a slice of an orange. Yuck! I still make the same face now that I did then. Then she would put Vaseline on our faces, so that the wind would not chap our skin. We were shiny but our faces didn't get cold!

I remember crying to her because I was tall and skinny and the boys called me "Sticks". She would comfort me and tell me her version of the Ugly Duckling story. When I became a teenager, she would call me her beautiful swan!

I remember one day when I was in high school and the boy I had a crush on looked at my chest and said, "Wow, I could put my hand on your back, and see it through your chest". I ran home and told my mother that I never wanted to wear a sweater again in life. She looked at me and pulled out an old picture of herself when she was a teenager. "No boobs," she said. "Look at me and look at the picture (her breasts were voluptuous). They will come." And of course they did!!!!!

I remember when she had to get up at 3:00 a.m. in the winter to catch the bus for work when she had the flu. Even though she was sick, she still came home, fixed dinner, helped me with my homework and got my clothes ready for me to go to school the next day.

When I worked my first job, my mother informed me that I had to donate to the house? Her explanation was, "You use the electricity, gas, water, my toilet tissue." What???? She took half of my money. I thought she was being mean and unfair. Then she told me that I would have to put 10% of my money in church, and save another 10% in a savings account. At that time, my savings account was a piggy bank! She also told me that from now on, I would have to buy my own clothes. Boy I was so pissed! I know now that she was teaching me how to become an adult, the value of money and the importance of self-reliance.

Why am I relating these stories to you? Because I want you to remember the times when the perception of your mother was what you thought it was supposed to be. But you should also remember that was what you needed then. If you think that you still need that validation, start looking at your own issues. Release the perception of who you think your mother is supposed to be and look realistically at who your mother is. When you release that perception, then think of your perception of who you are and who your mother needs you to be now. Don't wait until it's too late.

Responses To Online Survey

This non-scientific anonymous online survey was limited to 10 questions and there were 52 female respondents between the age of 40 and 70.

Do you see yourself in any of these responses? Compare these responses with your own.

Question 1.   How Old Are You
The age range of respondents was 49-70. The average age was 59.

Question 2.   How Old Is Your Mother Or Age Of Mother When She Passed.
The age range for mothers who are alive was 61-83. The average age of living mothers was 69. The age range of deceased mothers was 60-96 with the average age of mothers who had passed of 76.5.

Question 3.   Were You or Are You Your Mother's Caregiver?
No (36) Yes (17)

Question 4.   If You Answered Yes To Question 3, Did You Live In The Same Household?
No (43) Yes (8)

Question 5.   Rate Your Relationship With Your Mother As Superior, Excellent, Satisfactory, Or Unsatisfactory.
Superior (24) Excellent (10) Satisfactory (12) Unsatisfactory (6)

Questions 6-10 are some of the comments of the respondents. There were identical comments which are not included.

Question 6.   Please Explain The Reason For Your Rating.

Comments of respondents who related their relationship as superior

- She's an angel. My mother was my hero.
- I have always been able to turn to her and tell her anything and everything, without being judged.
- We were very similar and got along well, had similar interests. She was supportive of me.
- We were always best friends. We had a very loving relationship. I value so many things she taught me.
- We have always been very close. We talk every day and I visit her for long weekends at least once a month. She lives about 90 miles away. She is very independent. I did have to help when she broke her ankle and had eye surgery. She's fun and I so enjoy talking to her and hanging out. We go on a local weeklong family vacation and spend holidays together. I love and respect her very much. She is so valued and loved by me and my family. I like her advice. I enjoy hanging out with her friends.
- I live out of town but speak with her often and we make each other laugh. I see her as much as I can and we enjoy each other's company. I respect her and am thankful for her
- We enjoy each other's company and share common interests.

Comments of Respondents Who Rated Their Relationship As Excellent

- I have a very good relationship with my mom. We don't share deepest/darkest secrets or concerns, but we do talk and email frequently (I don't live near my parents) and I am able to visit every year or two.

- I live out of town but speak with her often and we make each other laugh. I see her as much as I can and we enjoy each other's company. I respect her and am thankful for her
- She has lived close to me for over 25 years and I am the one she depends on. I knew what she needed, gave her respect and allowed her to decide what she could and could not do.
- Sometimes we can both be rather stubborn but I love her anyway. While we did not always agree, we did always respect the opinions of the other.
- We are close and enjoy each other's company
- We live in different states and my sister is her caregiver.
- Both adult women, we give each other space. She is my biggest cheerleader.

Comments of Respondents Who Rated Their Relationship As Satisfactory

- We do have arguments, but in general we get along very well.
- I moved to CA from VA for a reason.
- We were very different people.
- She was not mentally competent when I cared for her and didn't know who I was.
- Mutual respect.
- We get along well but are not the closest.
- My parents divorced when I was a teenager and each remarried. My mother's new husband(s) have complicated my relationship with her.
- We were estranged for over 4 years. I had a very tumultuous life and upbringing.
- Hard to say. I thought my relationship was average. I didn't realize how much damage was caused.

Comments of Respondents Who Rated Their Relationship As Unsatisfactory

- My mother was abusive.
- We do not get along and I do not wish to change things.
- Tough childhood and she wasn't there a lot of the time.
- My mother was not a very good role model growing up. She is very selfish and opinionated.
- Had nothing to do with each other until she was dying then I was the one who stepped up to help.
- She was mean.
- I was never "close" with my mother - she preferred my sister.

Question 7.   What One Thing Does Your Mother Do/Say That Triggers Strong Negative/Positive Feelings?

- I'm used to them.
- Listen to me.
- She is self-centered and selfish.
- Gossip triggers negative feelings, praise triggers positive feelings.
- "I will wait for you." Was grateful and assured she would not die without me being there.
- She doesn't say anything that triggers negative feelings.
- Positive: She tells me she loves me every time we talk.
- Negative: If she's not happy with me, I can hear her coldness over the phone.
- She was hard on my children.
- She wants me to visit more often.
- She has dementia so nothing bugs me.
- She likes to criticize my lifestyle, my lack of a good career, etc., and liked my sister best.
- She complains, but it's to be expected.

- When she asks me what is wrong. I know she loves me and can tell something is wrong.
- She is a master of manipulation and negates my worth
- Have not spoken or seen her in 27 years.
- Always something medically wrong.
- She says, "I love you with all my heart."
- Negative: "I can't hear you. The phone is broken," when it's her not wanting to put in her hearing aids.
- She had Alzheimer's and it hurt knowing she didn't know who I was when she was in the last stages.
- Think. Let's make a game plan that you can live with.
- She tries to get me to talk to my older sister, after we had a falling out over 10 years ago.
- Frequently said that she never wanted children and hated us.
- My mom was a teacher. She understood kids. I feel blessed that she made time for my brother and me when we were kids. My mom smoked cigarettes and that has led me to work with a tobacco control program.
- She loves laying on guilt.
- I love when she tells me how much she enjoys visiting my home.
- When she wants me to fix my hair or clothes when it's not really necessary. Positive - being with her or talking on the phone - just being the fantastic, loving Mom that she is.
- My mother's lack of interest in being a grandparent can be difficult.
- Making someone happy.
- Obvious lack of interest; interested only in herself.
- Bragging up someone else's children and her closeness to my sister triggers negative feelings.

- Negative-when she doesn't listen to me. Positive-when we enjoy the same things.
- 'Some days chickens, some days feathers" always makes me remember that life is full of ups and downs, makes me smile.
- I hated it when she acted old.
- Sometimes too opinionated.
- She keeps bringing up details of her marriage to my father, which makes me feel bad e.g., If only your dad had...
- She always encouraged me to do wonderful, adventurous things in order to be who I wanted to be.
- Critical of me. Doesn't nurture. JUDGEMENTAL. Never there for me. Not a close relationship ever.
- She has very liberal feelings towards things.
- Unsolicited advice, and criticism makes me feel bad and she always corrects my grammar.
- Nothing really, she can just be annoying. I have a much better relationship with her now that I don't see her as often.

Question 8.   If You Feel That There Were More Negative Feelings, How Do You Cope?

- EFT, essential oils and most importantly, prayer & forgiveness.
- Concentrate on the state of her mind.
- My parents divorced when I was ten. Divorce wasn't very common in small-town American in the early 70s so there were never any discussions/explanations given to us kids. Still bothered by that somewhat, but not enough to upset my mom by asking her questions. She did the best she could at the time, and you really can never ask for more than that.

- There are no negative feelings.
- I remind myself that she is an individual and free to make her own choices.
- I know it isn't her and realizing that she's human.
- I'm just pretty much going to ignore them and change the topic.
- I shut down. Depression. Worthlessness.
- I don't cope - I don't see her.
- Not a problem anymore, my mother is deceased.
- Because I have MS I have to stay away from toxic emotions, so when she tries to manipulate me I have to not buy into it. The more upset I get the faster I die. With Multiple Sclerosis, stress can kill you real fast.
- I knew she could not control herself and was dying. I just wanted her to be as comfortable as possible.
- The negative would have to be my own guilty feelings for not having thought something through.
- Mom did not put out negative vibes.
- I talk to my husband about it.
- Just let it go.
- My mom has been gone for 17 years. There are no negative feelings. I wish she had had some of the tobacco cessation tools that we have now. It may have changed the course of her life and given her more time with us and allowed her to meet her other two grandkids.
- Learned to not accept the guilt and told her so.
- I speak with my brother and sisters.
- I try not to think negative thoughts.
- I try not to mull over them; sing Zippi-dee-doo-dah three times as punishment.
- I ignore.
- I moved away so as not to be near my family.
- I take deep breaths.

- I express my concerns by using "I" statements, e.g. I feel sad, etc.
- I miss my mother now that she's gone. I cope by remembering how lucky I am to have had her in my life.
- I go to therapy and I keep my distance from my mother. I accept it will never be the way I deserve. I focus on being a loving, nurturing, affectionate mom to my daughter.
- Personally my glass has always been overflowing. I try to help others see the more positive aspects of life.
- I share with my husband to get it out of my system.
- I usually take a walk.

Question 9: If You Feel That There Were More Positive Feelings, To What Do You Attribute That?

- Her patience, and she was a good mother.
- Like I said, she was a great lady. I never had any doubt that I was loved.
- We both try to look at the positives in life - almost every time I talk to her I laugh, or at least hang up the phone with a smile on my face.
- My Christian upbringing.
- God working in my life
- I remember our history and all she did for me.
- Compassion, empathy, and her kindness to others.
- Stress factors or my mother's mood that particular day. I am a positive person. I realize that everyone has bad days, and don't dwell on the negative things.
- We have a lot in common. Many of the same interests.
- Positive attitudes; acceptance of anything.
- 3 years of good therapy.
- Our long relationship and her knowing I only have so much to give.

- I did a good job caring for her.
- She was the oldest of 12 children and learned to take life as it comes at a very early age.
- My mom was a very optimistic person. Her glass was always half full. She instilled values of service, hard work, hard play, and community spirit. I look to these assets for inspiration and I attribute this to my positive outlook on life, too.
- A closeness that we have always shared. Mutual respect.
- Because we love each other very much.
- We are mature and have common values.
- I have a wonderful mother, and we have a very meaningful relationship.
- I am unsure if there are more positive feelings than other feelings. It's mostly okay, but nothing more.
- Assisting people.
- My determination to feel positive toward her.
- Living close to each other.
- Having the same tastes in food, travel, and cultural events.
- My mother was an incredible woman who easily shared her view of life and always stood by her children, but never overindulged them.
- She was a great person and we got along well.
- Open and honest and clear communication and respect for each other as individuals.
- She was a very kind, good person. I never doubted her love.
- I don't. We don't have a good relationship at all.
- I am a positive person.
- My pregnancy.
- She was a pretty good mom overall.
- Being sensitive to each other's feelings

- Intelligence

Question 10:   Additional Comments

- I loved my mother, but she didn't know who I was because of Alzheimer's.
- You make me cry just thinking about her. I miss her.
- I hope and pray my parents (my mom and stepdad) will not need a caregiver but if that changes I will do whatever I need to do to be there for them.
- My mother grew up in a very different environment and air than I did so we will always have different ideas on many different topics. In general we get along fine and I love her.
- While growing up we fought often, but as I grew older, I understood what a great mother she is to me and began to really appreciate her.
- She taught me great lessons in life for my family. She was a magnificent woman!
- In the past I have had to limit my contact with negative people – some in my family and some who think my MS is not happening. They think it's all in my head. My brother, for instance. Since he became a reborn Christian he has gotten to be a narrow-minded, mean, hateful person who I have to shun, currently. He disagrees with every little thing, interferes with the care I give my mom, although he is thousands of miles away and does nothing to help the situation.
- I miss mom so very much.
- Middle child of five kids and only one who had nothing to do with my mother until she was dying
- My mom was brilliant, witty and a lot of fun. She loved books and fast cars and spiked hot chocolate. She made

time for others and still kept us as her priority. Miss her like crazy, even after 17 years.

- We have always shown our love first.
- We let go of old stories.
- Mom is deceased, but our last years together we grew back together. Perhaps it was my age, but I was able to finally see the sorrow she lived with, just as I had. I will miss her.
- I am so very lucky to have the giving, loving, fun, smart mother that I have.
- Only saw her twice in my teens - early 20's.
- Not easy at times but glad I can be home to take care of her.
- If every mother was like mine, the world would be a much better place. Love always.
- We have a lifetime of shared memories. She did the best she could.
- It's very sad to live 42 years feeling you were never wanted by your mother.
- I love my mother. She lost her mother and I lost my sister so we have each other to lean and depend on.
- Mom worked all her life, so she was hardly around to establish a close relationship.
- I'm glad she's still around.
- When caring for someone you must recognize what you can do and cannot do. If you cannot do it you must seek outside help.

End of Survey

Understanding Your Mother's Fear of Being Cast Aside

As my mother gets older, I can see that she is increasingly unable to take care of herself. I have approached her about living with me and my husband, but I hear, "You will try to run my life and tell me what to do." I just chuckle when she says that. However, I found out that when my brother talks to her about living with me, she often tells him that she knows that I don't want her with me because she would be a burden. I am sure that many of you have heard the same words. I am also sure that a few of you probably agree. But it is important when healing your relationship that you empathize with your mother and if it becomes necessary for that living arrangement to take place, that you make them feel needed, loved and a blessing instead of a burden. Health problems can impact moms' behavior - loss of mobility, incontinence, balance, vision & hearing loss, frustration, depression, anger, confusion, memory loss, and feelings of isolation.

Conflicts often happen in the relationship between mothers and daughters because, subconsciously, mothers want their daughters to follow in their footsteps. This may be career-wise, the way they view the world, their choice in life partners, the way they raise their children, etc.

Who Is Yo' Mama?

According to, Loving Your Parents When They Can No Longer Love You, written by Terry Hargraves, There are four types of seniors.

1. The type who accepts the fact that they are aging and can't do the things they used to do. This type is usually pleasant to be around.

2. The type who refuses to accept that they are aging with its constraints. This type is usually defensive, angry and although they may need help, they usually refuse assistance.

3. The type who feels sorry for themselves and wants you to pity them and often wants someone to take care of them.

4. The type who submits to the challenges of aging, and becomes passive and depressed.

I discovered that according to these 4 types, my mother is a combination of numbers 2 and 3. Most of the time, she feels that she can still do the things she did when she was much younger. Even though it is obvious at times that she needs help, she refuses it. Although your mom may exhibit all four of these types of behavior at one time or another, you may see more of one type of behavior. If you think about it, even you can exhibit anyone of these behaviors. Therefore, whatever type she is, remember to be more patient, understanding and compassionate.

Communication Commandments

Rhonda H. Kelley in her book, Raising Mom, discussed what she called the Ten Commandments For Communication. They included having a regular time and day to have conversations with your mother so that she will begin to expect your call. I call my mother every Monday afternoon. She likes to talk about what happened at church on Sunday. I make sure that I have plenty of time just in case she wants to have a long conversation.

When you speak to her, remember that she is coming from a different generation with different values and experiences. Therefore, there will probably be plenty of times when she will not understand why you do things differently or think differently.

Don't be impatient when speaking with her. At times she may want to have a long conversation or she may have difficulty forming her thoughts.

Consider her emotions when you are having your conversation. This is a hard one. Try not to take some of the things she says personally. Don't try to read between the lines.

Do not give unwanted advice or make decisions for her without asking her opinion. Remember how you felt when your mother gave you advice that you did not ask for? You usually rebelled. Wait for her to ask for your opinion. Remember, she may respond just like you did when you were a teenager.

Completely ignore the advice or do exactly the opposite! My mother was having a difficult time remembering what pills to take and when to take them. I took it upon myself to get her a daily pill box, and put the pills in them. When I checked the pill box the next week, pills were still in them. I asked her why she was not using it. Her reply was, "You didn't ask me if I wanted one."

When you have concerns about some decisions that your mom may be making, make sure you have real, actual evidence to defend your concerns. My mother's beautician died and she had to find another one. The person who was recommended lived down the street from her apartment, but there was a busy street that had to be crossed. My mom walks with a walker and walks very slowly. She was determined to walk to this beautician on her own. The only way I could convince her not to do that was to remind her of two of the senior tenants in her building that had been hit by cars trying to cross that busy street.

If you have specific things that you want to talk to your mother about, write them down. You can't remember everything. Making a list is helpful and will relieve frustration for you, especially if (after you talk with her), there were some important things that you forgot to say.

If at all possible, think ahead to help your mother. Some of her needs may be unpredictable, but routine needs are easy to anticipate. I go to the grocery store for my mother and she does not always think of everything she needs. I made a list of all of the foods she eats, put it on an excel spread sheet, and notate the dates the items were bought. This allows me to anticipate her grocery needs, and saves me from a lot of daily trips to the grocery store.

Make sure your mother has other people she can have conversations with when you are not available. If you can, foster relationships with church members that are her age, impress on her the importance of keeping up with her friends. If there are other family members, e.g., grandchildren, brothers, sisters, etc., let them know when you are not available and ask them to make sure they call and talk with her.

Lordy, Lordy, I Have Become My Mother

In a new memoir, Brooke Shields chronicles the ups-and-downs of her late mother's constant presence and untiring devotion. The book is entitled, There Was a Little Girl: The Real Story of My Mother and Me, published by Penguin Group. According to The Associated Press, it is an insightful read from beginning to end. She speaks about her relationship with her mother. In essence, Brooke talks about seeing her mother in herself.

What do you think and feel when people begin to tell you that you look like, sound like, act like, your mother? When they hear you on the phone and say, "Oh, I thought you were your mom." Or when they say you're just like your mom with the same mannerisms and reactions. What about the times you hear yourself saying to your children, the same things your mother said to you. The older we become, the more often we look in our mirrors and at photographs and recognize we look and sound just like our mothers. Sometimes we are happy about it and sometimes we are not.

Well, I can tell you what I said. "No, I'm not!" Usually that's what most of us say when we are told that we have turned into our mothers. But just think about it, is that all bad? Well sometimes it is and sometimes it isn't. Some of our behaviors and beliefs that we inherited from our mothers are undesirable and may even be destructive. My mother was very controlling. And I hated her control, even when I knew she was right. I swore that I would not have a control freak personality. Well, my husband says I am a control freak! My friends say I'm a control freak! My colleagues say I'm a control freak! OK, OK, OK, maybe I am!!!!

Let's look at what we admire about our mothers. I decided to take inventory. How am I like my mother? My mom is a very independent, self-sufficient woman. After my father left, she had to raise four boys and one girl alone, and was a pretty strict disciplinarian. The boys were mostly compliant, but I was headstrong.

My mother read a lot, and placed the joy of reading into me. She used to read me stories when I was little and when I became able to read, she bought me classic books. Little Women and Black Beauty were my two favorites.

My mother loved music, had a beautiful voice and used to sing around the house when she was cleaning. She always bought very fine conservative clothes, loved shoes (which were usually the latest styles). People would refer to her as a sharp dresser. As a matter of fact, some of her friends were a little jealous of the way she dressed. She belonged to several organizations both social and civic, was a dedicated member of her church, and loved to travel. WOW! Am I looking in a mirror?

I even find myself with the same habits. When I was growing up, I hated it when my mother would make me wash the dishes right after dinner or clean up as we were preparing a meal. Her favorite quote was, "You clean up as you go along." I swore that when I became grown and had my own kitchen, I would wash dishes the next morning. So what do I find myself doing? By the time we are sitting down to dinner, I have already washed the utensils I used to cook, and after dinner, you would not be able to tell that a dinner had been eaten; everything washed, and food put away! I'll ask again, is that all bad?

In the end, we are our mother's daughters. We have behaviors, talents and dreams just like them, but we also have our individualities. We can't help being influenced by our mothers, even if it's unintentional. Our mothers are our first models for being women. Of course not everything our mothers pass down must be thrown out. A lot of what she has imbedded in us must be kept.

Working Things Out

Why is this mother/daughter relationship considered so complicated? It takes patience on both parts, along with vulnerability, acceptance and understanding. You don't have to agree on everything. Don't get caught in an I-am-right-you-are-wrong mindset. Your perspectives and strengths are completely different. While at times it may feel hopeless and frustrating, you can gain a deeper understanding and a new appreciation for each other.

Becoming a teenager, I was searching for my own identity and there was bound to be conflict. My mother wanted my hair long. I wanted my hair short. I cut my hair. She was very critical until my hair grew back out. I wanted her approval, but I was developing as my own person with my own agenda. I was determined to be me! Our relationship was definitely a work in progress.

It's hard for a controlling type of mother to let go. This type of mother doesn't like admitting that her daughter is becoming an adult and is capable of thinking and acting on her own behalf. We look to our parents for guidance and want to admire them for their knowledge. Our mothers are significant to our future relationships and influence who we are and who or what we want to be. They are not perfect. They had their ideas of what kind of lives they wanted us to live. We look at our mothers' traits and make decisions about what we want to keep and what we want to leave behind. When we reach our twenties or thirties, we usually become aware of these inherited traits. This is when we begin the selection process.

What qualities and practices are you going to continue carrying on, and what are you going to let go? We have to pick and choose which decisions to follow and which mistakes to avoid in order to discover what's true for us. We have both positive and negative kinds of baggage from past generations, but we don't have to carry all of it indefinitely, especially if pain comes with it.

We are our mother's daughters and for that, there is nothing but appreciativeness and perhaps a little sadness. Remember, you were created out of your mother's body, and there should be happiness in that.

You Are A Good Daughter

You are a good daughter. If you have loved your mother enough to feel the pain of her hurting you, and the pain of you hurting her, you are a good daughter. If you have tried to forgive her, even if you haven't been able to so far, you are a good daughter. If you have ever striven to do the very best that you can, even under challenging circumstances, you are a good daughter.

And it's okay. It's okay if your relationship was challenging. It's okay if your relationship was awful. It's okay if you said or did things that you aren't proud of, of which you are ashamed, or that you wish you could take back. It's okay.

Guilt is among the most visceral of human emotions. Too often, because of its very nature, we push it down until it becomes a near-permanent part of us. It becomes something that rattles around in the background at all times and then, every so often, flares up painfully like a chronic illness that our immune systems suppress, but can't quite shake. I believe it takes a lot of soothing, deep breathing and self-forgiving, again and again and again, to heal your guilt. Especially if you are grieving, because guilt is so painful and cuts so deeply that it is well known to be an integral part of grief.

So I will say it again. Because I want you to know it so much that you feel it in your bones and your heart and your teeth and your skin and every part of you that hurts.

You are a good daughter.

You are a good daughter. And it's okay.
Rebecca Emily Darling

The Hand That Rocks The Cradle

I thought I would include this poem to remind us of how important mothers are. I often wonder why there isn't a lot of research about the mother daughter relationship. Let's look at this. The mother has a daughter; the daughter becomes a mother and so on and so on and so on. As this poem points out, one of the most important interpersonal relationships is the relationship a daughter has with her mother. This relationships affects all other relationships be they personal, professional, etc. In my opinion, there should be mandatory classes for women who have daughters.

William Ross Wallace (1819-1881)
THE HAND THAT ROCKS THE CRADLE IS
THE HAND THAT RULES THE WORLD.
BLESSINGS on the hand of women!
   Angels guard its strength and grace.
In the palace, cottage, hovel,
   Oh, no matter where the place;
Would that never storms assailed it,
   Rainbows ever gently curled,
For the hand that rocks the cradle
   Is the hand that rules the world.
Infancy's the tender fountain,
   Power may with beauty flow,
Mothers first to guide the streamlets,
   From them souls unresting grow—
Grow on for the good or evil,
   Sunshine streamed or evil hurled,
For the hand that rocks the cradle
   Is the hand that rules the world.
Woman, how divine your mission,
   Here upon our natal sod;

Keep—oh, keep the young heart open
  Always to the breath of God!
All true trophies of the ages
  Are from mother-love impearled,
For the hand that rocks the cradle
  Is the hand that rules the world.
Blessings on the hand of women!
  Fathers, sons, and daughters cry,
And the sacred song is mingled
  With the worship in the sky—
Mingles where no tempest darkens,
  Rainbows evermore are hurled;
For the hand that rocks the cradle
  Is the hand that rules the world.

Contradictions

How can your mother be so proud of you on one hand and belittle you on the other? Annette told me her story.

"She would often introduce me to her acquaintances very proudly, and whenever I had an accomplishment in my career, she would tell everyone how proud she was of me. But when we were alone, I received no validation from her. In fact, it was just the opposite – "So you did it. So what?" One day, I asked her about this contradiction. Our conversation was very enlightening. She told me the story of how she was always a very smart student and wanted to go to college. Her grandmother paid for her for to go away for two years. She was always on the Dean's List, but in her junior year, her mother refused to send her back. Her grandmother promised to pay for the rest of her college education, but her mother refused to let her go. She said she was very hurt about it, never forgave her mother, and felt that this prevented her from having the life she wanted to live. She then told me that she was very proud of me and didn't mean to belittle my accomplishments. However, sometimes it brought up those old feelings of how she wasn't allowed to finish college. Those feelings made her say things that she really didn't mean. She asked for my forgiveness. Of course I forgave her, even though it would still happen from time to time.

Toya, an acquaintance, told me about how competition between she and her mother manifested itself in contradictions. Toya is an accomplished musician, has a beautiful voice and her own band. Toya feels that her talents came from her mom, who also has a beautiful singing voice. Toya and her band travel around the world, playing at different venues. She often has her mother accompany her when her band is going out of the country. When they return, her mother brags to her friends about how wonderful her trips are, how talented her daughter is, and how she appreciates being able to travel out of the country.

However, Toya said that her mother has never told that to her directly.

One day, at a local venue, Toya asked her mother to join her on the stage for a duet. Her mother not only sang louder that Toya, she nudged Toya aside and took center stage. When Toya spoke to her about it, her mother said she just got overexcited and said that it wouldn't happen again. Would Toya please let her sing with her at the next local venue? The second time, her mother did the same thing. When Toya asked her about it, her mother said, "Remember, you got your talent from me, it's obvious that I sing better than you, always have and always will."

I related my story to Toya, and she remembered that her mother wanted to be an entertainer, but got married and had children instead. "I know she is proud of me, but I guess in the back of her mind, she has a little resentment that it's me instead of her. I'm still going to ask her to join me on stage from time to time, but I think next time, I will let her lead the song."

I saw Toya a few months later and asked her how things were going. She told me that she did let her mother lead a song, and her mother has been floating on a cloud ever since. One night after Toya's performance, her mother pulled her aside, hugged her, and told her how proud she was of her and said, "You do sing much better than me!"

Support Systems

It is very important for you to have a support system. A support system can consist of trusted friends, family members, and/or your religious leader. My support system includes my husband, my best friend, one of my mom's friends, and my life coach. My best girlfriend is always there when I need to vent or need a shoulder to cry on. She gives me validation in that she says to me, "When your mother is called home, you should have no regrets. You have been a good daughter." She has told me that when we were younger she admired the relationship I had with my mother. She saw that we travelled together, shopped together, and always seemed to enjoy each other's company.

She reminds me that my mother is older, feels her mortality, and is fighting for her independence. Of course, my husband is very supportive, because he was the caretaker for his mother until Alzheimer's disease forced him to place her in a nursing home.

I have other friends who have gone through similar situations with their mothers and they impress upon me to have patience and stay in prayer. My mother's doctor frequently tells me how much she admires my patience and willingness to always look after my mother's well-being.

Make sure you have someone to talk to when you are stressed or frustrated and even when there are times that you want to celebrate the good times with your mother.

Sisters & Mothers

One young lady shared a story regarding her relationship with her mother and her three sisters. Pat is the second oldest of eight children and she and her mother had a very close relationship. Pat knew that her sisters resented her for this close relationship, but her sisters usually kept that resentment quiet. Now that the mother is ill, Pat's sisters overtly demonstrate their jealousy. Negative comments come from out of the blue towards Pat for no apparent reason. Pat always knew that if there came a time when her mother would have to be taken care of, she would be the one to do it. Her mother is bedridden and it seems that Pat's sisters have turned into the stepsisters from the Cinderella story. The following is how Pat describes herself and her sisters.

Pat: Second oldest daughter of eight children; laid back; opinionated but will not argue; responsible and giving; considered Mom a parent and a friend; and willing to listen and compromise to help keep down conflict. Pat is usually on the opposite side of her sisters when making decisions. She doesn't always express her feelings and views to avoid confrontation and to avoid prolonging unending, unnecessary arguments.

Annete: Third oldest daughter of eight children; likes to be in control; always comes to the aid when someone is in trouble, even for people she doesn't like. She looks for people to need her and they have to do what she wants or tells them to do in order to get her help or support. If you do not follow her lead she will keeping coming back telling you how it should be done, change things behind your back, constantly correct you, tell you, "You missed a spot. I do it like this" or simply ignore you and do it her way. Volunteers to help but always says she's tired, always serious, takes every opportunity to get away. In 2015 alone, she took 6 trips - California, Peoria, and about 4 trips to Washington.

Sheila (She-She): Sixth child, fourth daughter of eight. Her only focus is on herself and her daughters. In her eyesight, no one is more beautiful or more intelligent than her daughters, and they are never wrong. Her favorite stories and only conversations are about her daughters. She-She and Annette consider themselves to be best friends and often confide in each other. Part of this relationship is because She-She and her daughters receive support from Annette. She-She can be lively and humorous. But is known to have mood swings and will turn on you in a minute. She does for Mom, but has let it be known that once she no longer has to, she will not be around.

Cheri: The youngest. She is the neatest and most anal of all of us. She is another version of Annette but in many ways is worse. She constantly checks behind you, only telling you what you did wrong or what you forgot to do. Example - with all the things we have to do, work, deal with family and take care of our own lives, Cheri, who works from 2-10, will come in and see that you did everything to her standards. The major difference between her and Annette is that Cheri is very outspoken and feels she should tell people how she feels about any and everything. She will argue on and on unless you are in agreement. If she loses, she will find someone to agree with her and will come back to you when she finds that person.

These family dynamics have led to verbal arguments, disagreements regarding mother's care, health care providers leaving because of the family's discord, and an atmosphere that is not conducive to our mother's health.

This poem was sent to me by my friend, Kathy.

Letter From A Mother To A Daughter:

"My dear girl, the day you see I'm getting old, I ask you to please be patient, but most of all, try to understand what I'm going through.

If when we talk, I repeat the same thing a thousand times, don't interrupt to say: "You said the same thing a minute ago"... Just listen, please. Try to remember the times when you were little and I would read the same story night after night until you would fall asleep.

When I don't want to take a bath, don't be mad and don't embarrass me. Remember when I had to run after you making excuses and trying to get you to take a shower when you were just a girl?

When you see how ignorant I am when it comes to new technology, give me the time to learn and don't look at me that way... remember, honey, I patiently taught you how to do many things like eating appropriately, getting dressed, combing your hair and dealing with life's issues every day... the day you see I'm getting old, I ask you to please be patient, but most of all, try to understand what I'm going through.

If I occasionally lose track of what we're talking about, give me the time to remember, and if I can't, don't be nervous, impatient or arrogant. Just know in your heart that the most important thing for me is to be with you.

And when my old, tired legs don't let me move as quickly as before, give me your hand the same way that I offered mine to you when you first walked.

When those days come, don't feel sad... just be with me, and understand me while I get to the end of my life with love. I'll cherish and thank you for the gift of time and joy we shared. With a big smile and the huge love I've always had for you, I just want to say, I love you... my darling daughter."

- Unknown

Recognition

As your mother grows older, you may start to see some behaviors that are foreign or very different to you. Your mother may ask you the same question many different times, you may see personality changes, or changes in some habits. If this is a concern to you, you may have to consider that your mother is showing the signs of early dementia or Alzheimer's disease. Your best bet would be to speak with her doctor who would be most able to recognize the symptoms. So, how will you manage? You must have patience, understanding, and seek professional support if necessary. Here is an excerpt from my friend Renee whose mother was diagnosed with Alzheimer's.

Breakfast With My Mom
by Renee Garner Elm

My mom was finally diagnosed with Dementia/Alzheimer's in 2009. I knew long before that date that something was changing and was wrong with how she prepared to cook, seasoned and picked the pots and pans for her meals and more importantly, how she prepared the simple meal of breakfast for her and my dad, which she did every morning. Somewhere in early 2007, my mom began to burn everything! She could prepare breakfast – usually 4 eggs, 6 pieces of bacon or sausage, 4 pieces of toast, rice or grits and 2 cups of coffee for her and my dad with her eyes closed!

Everything would come out perfectly done all at the same time with no effort shown whatsoever. Then various things would burn as she forgot they were on behind her – skillets, pots, toast, etc. That's when we started the ritual of going out to breakfast a few days a week. Just the three of us! If that did not happen, I would come over and make breakfast for them and we would all eat together. When my dad was in a nursing home, I spent the evenings with my mom and would wake up and fix breakfast for her every day.

As the Alzheimer's got worse and my mom became more sensitive to sounds, the minute I put my feet on the floor, my mom would spring out of bed and ask, "Are you going to fix breakfast?" My mom and dad were always early risers, so they did not ever rely on the sun to get the day started.

Every day, I would say, "Yes I am, mom. Are you hungry?"

She would reply, "Girl, yes!! I'll get dressed." She would put on whatever clothes I left out from the day before or come up with her own combination of things, but she sat at the kitchen table or in front of the TV in her same spot every day and this became our new pattern or morning ritual.

One morning, I was extremely tired and thought that if I just remained still, I could sleep a little longer and that my mom would not get up until my feet hit the floor. I heard the door creek and knew she was looking at me with her hands on her hips. When I opened my eyes, she had her hands on her hips, her head was leaning to the left and she said with a smile and stern look, "Are you going to sleep all day, or are you going to make me some breakfast?" Then we both laughed so hard, we were crying and holding our stomachs for 10 minutes!

I replied as soon as I could speak, "Yes, ma'am! I will get your breakfast right away before its lunch time!" We laughed all the way to the kitchen together – arm in arm! I said, "I love you mama!"

She said, "I love you too! You take such good care of me!"

I replied to her, "That is all that I know how to do is to take good care of you like you take good care of me." I loved that time with my mom. I was unemployed but never wanted for anything. Our time together was priceless.

Is It Me Or Is It Her?

I'm including a letter that was sent to me by a young lady who lives with her mother. When I told her I was writing a book about mother daughter relationships, she wanted to share her story.

Here are my mother's situations. I don't know if it's aging, brain surgery or both. Either way, she is getting on my nerves!

1. She expects me to remember stuff from months ago. When she asks me such questions, I try to calmly tell her I don't remember, which I don't. When she persists and I get irritated, she'll hear it in my voice and let it go.

2. She keeps asking me the same stuff over and over within a few days' time. STOP IT!

3. She has a tablet, laptop and iPod touch and still expects me to look stuff up on the Internet. And she wants me to address it even when I'm in the middle of working on something.

4. She's become a church gossip and doesn't even go to that church anymore.

5. She will not clean up my living room! So my living room has paper strewn across the floor and living room, which is annoying as hell because I cleaned up. One day she said, "I don't move as fast as I used to." I told her that it's been three months and all she has to do it take time to do it and it will be done within a few hours.

6. I work from home. She'll call me from another room and I may be on a business call.

7. She'll come into my office in the morning talking about nothing when she knows that's my spiritual and writing time. Go away already!

8. I'm always leery when she asks me what I'm doing each day. I now respond, "Why?"

9. She'll text me from her classes saying how much stuff she has to bring home instead of asking for a ride home. I used to offer rides. Now, when she sends those texts I say, "Ok". If she wants a ride, she has to ask.

10. She'll ask, "Do you want to do/go _____?" No, I don't. I told her the better way to make that request is, "I want to do/go _____ and would like for you to do/go with me."

11. One day we wanted a rotisserie chicken from a local store. Because the store didn't have any, I went to 3 different stores, that war further away and waited for hours for the chicken. When I returned, she asked, "Why didn't you buy a chicken from the local store?" Really? Do you think I would have passed buying a bird from the first store to come to the hood for food? That irked me.

Years ago I used to feel bad about saying no to my mother but it's so much easier now because I value my time differently. I used to give up stuff I wanted to do for stuff she wanted to do. That's not happening any more.

Readers, what do you think about Mom's actions and Jeannette's reactions? Blog me and let me know.

Awareness

As our mothers get older, there is a chance that she might begin to suffer from dementia or Alzheimer's disease. If and when that time comes, patience, understanding, prayer and support - both medical and otherwise - will be important. I can see now that my mom might have been suffering from some of these symptoms, and I was unaware. Here are ten early warning signs to look for.

1. Memory loss that interrupts daily life, e.g., asking the same question over and over.
2. Challenges in planning or solving problems, e.g., increasing difficulty in keeping track of monthly bills.
3. Difficulty completing familiar tasks, e.g., having a hard time remembering the rules of a favorite card game.
4. Time or place confusion, e.g., forgetting how a destination was reached.
5. Difficulty understanding visual images and spatial relationships, e.g., trouble reading.
6. New problems with spoken or written words, e.g., repeating words or trouble understanding familiar words.
7. Misplacing things and losing the ability to retrace steps, e.g., putting things in unusual places.
8. Decreased or poor judgment, e.g., paying less attention to personal grooming.
9. Withdrawal from work or social activities, e.g., avoiding social situations.
10. Changes in mood and personality, e.g., confusion, fearfulness, anxiousness, depression or anger.

Occasional forgetfulness may be typical due to a lack of sleep or even dehydration many of us experience from time to time. However, if you consistently notice any of these symptoms, become your mother's best health advocate and make an appointment for her to see the doctor.

According to the Alzheimer's Association, in 2015 an estimated 5.3 million Americans of all ages have Alzheimer's, and the number is expected to grow each year as the population of Americans age 65 and older grows.

Caregiving

The average caregiver is a 49 year old woman, caring for her 60 year old mother who does not live with her. She is married and employed. [Updated February 2015] 88 AARP (2011). Valuing the Invaluable 2011 update.. Retrieved (January 10, 2015) fromhttp://assets.aarp.org/rgcenter/ppi/ltc/fs229-ltc.pdf In 2005, one in nine older women aged 75+ and one in five aged 85 or older, needed assistance with daily activities.1313 AARP Public Policy Institute. (2005) National Health Interview Survey. Retrieved (January 2015) fromhttp://www.aarp.org/home-garden/livable-communities/info-2007/fs77r_ltc.html [Updated February 2015]

One national study on women and caregiving highlighted the conflicting demands of work and eldercare. MetLife Mature Market Institute, National Alliance for Caregiving, & The National Center on Women and Aging. (1999, November). The MetLife juggling act study on balancing caregiving with work and the costs involved. Below are some statistics.

- 33% of working women decreased work hours
- 29% passed up a job promotion, training or assignment
- 22% took a leave of absence
- 20% switched from full-time to part-time employment
- 16% quit their jobs
- 13% retired early

The same study found that women who cared for ill parents were twice as likely to suffer from depressive or anxious symptoms as non-caregivers. Pavalko, E. K., & Artis, J. E. (1997). Women's caregiving and paid work: Causal relationships in late midlife. Journal of Gerontology: Social Sciences, 52B (4), 170–179.

Bottom Line

The bottom line is that some of us have difficult relationships with our mothers and some of us don't. Hopefully, if you are in the former group, you have found something in this book that resonates with you and will help you forge a better relationship with your mother.

You won't change your mother, but you can change how you respond to any situation. It takes mindfulness and practice and it's not going to happen overnight. My suggestion is to have a strategy, share with your friends who are in the same situation, ask for advice, laugh and BREATHE! Vision boards are often used for people who want a visible example of a goal they want to reach. You can put pictures of mothers and daughters in positive situations, quotes, Scriptures, etc. On a personal note, I put the words of two old songs, Happy Days Are Here Again and a take-off on the song, I Love My Baby, My Baby Loves Me. I substitute "baby" for "mother" on my vision board, and also sing one of them quietly in my mind when my mother and I are in a conflictual situation. Believe it or not, it helps!

I saved the best strategy for last - PRAYER. Prayer changes things. It will not only help you in your place, it can change the dynamics of your relationship. Below are some scriptures worth remembering.

For if you forgive people their wrongdoing, your heavenly Father will forgive you as well.
Matthew 6:14

Therefore, as God's chosen people, holy and dearly loved, clothe yourselves with compassion, kindness, humility, gentleness and patience. Bear with each other and forgive one another if any of you has a grievance against someone. Forgive as the Lord

forgave you. And over all these virtues put on love, which binds them all together in perfect unity.
Colossians 3:12-14

Behold, everyone who uses proverbs will use this proverb about you: 'Like mother, like daughter.'
Ezekiel 16:44

Her children rise up and call her blessed; her husband also, and he praises her.
Proverbs 31:28 ESV

If one curses his father or his mother, his lamp will be put out in utter darkness.
Proverbs 20:20 ESV

Listen to your father who gave you life, and do not despise your mother when she is old.......... let her who bore you rejoice.
Proverbs
23:22-25 ESV

Love is patient and kind; love does not envy or boast; it is not arrogant or rude. It does not insist on its own way; it is not irritable or resentful; it does not rejoice at wrongdoing, but rejoices with the truth. Love bears all things, believes all things, hopes all things, and endures all things.
1 Corinthians 13:4-7

Be Blessed

Resources

1. Evans-Williams, Venus 3 Steps To Healing A Strained Mother-Daughter Relationship, June 11, 2013

2. Fingerman KL. Tight lips?: Aging mothers' and adult daughters' responses to interpersonal tensions in their relationships. Personal Relationships. 1998; 5:121–138.

3. Hargraves. Terry "Loving Your Parents when They Can No Longer Love You" Zondervan; 1st edition (March 1, 2005) ...

4. Jakes, T.D "Mothers and Daughters" YouTube video

5. Kelley, Rhonda H. "Raising Moms" Daughters caring for mothers in their later years, new hope publishers, Birmingham, AL pp 97-101

6. Mintel, Linda "I Love My Mother But..." Practical Help to Get the Most Out of Your Relationship. Harvest House Publishers, Eugene Oregon 2004.

7. Moninger, Jeannette "Relaxation Techniques that zap Stress Fast" Reviewed by Michael w. Smith, M.D, WebMD Feature

8. Pavalko, E. K., & Artis, J. E. (1997). Women's caregiving and paid work: Causal relationships in late midlife. Journal of Gerontology: Social Sciences, 52B (4), 170–179.

9. Ryff CD1, Lee YH, Essex MJ, Schmutte PS. My children and me: midlife evaluations of grown children and of self. Psychol Aging. 1994

10. Sidell, Robert "The Gateway, Discover the Power to Create an Outrageously Prosperous and Happy Life".

11. Tracy, Laura, Ph.D. "Our Mothers, Ourselves: Mother-Daughter Relationships." *HowStuffWorks*. N.p., 25 May 2005.